# Justice Denied

There is a silent epidemic of childhood sexual abuse in the United States, and a legal system that is not effectively protecting children from predators. Recent coverage of widespread abuse in the public schools and in churches has brought the once-taboo subject of childhood sexual abuse to the forefront. The problem extends well beyond schools and churches, though: the vast majority of survivors are sexually abused by family or family acquaintances with 90 percent of abuse never reported to the authorities. Despite increasing awareness of the problem, current law does little to identify predators. Popular legal fixes, like sex offender registries, increased sentences, and pedophile-free zones, are ineffective without that knowledge. Marci A. Hamilton proposes a comprehensive yet simple solution: eliminate the arbitrary statutes of limitations for childhood sexual abuse so that survivors past and present can get into court. Most states have such short statutes of limitations that survivors cannot get to court before the doors are locked shut. Removing this arbitrary barrier would permit survivors to unmask their perpetrators, and open a path to justice and public vindication. Standing in the way, however, are formidable opponents such as the insurance industry and the hierarchy of the Roman Catholic Church.

In *Justice Denied*, Hamilton predicts a coming civil rights movement for children and explains why it is in the interest of all Americans to allow victims of childhood sexual abuse this chance to seek justice *when they are ready*.

Marci A. Hamilton is one of the United States' leading church/state scholars, as well as an expert on federalism and representation. Hamilton is Visiting Professor of Public Affairs at the Woodrow Wilson School and the Kathleen and Martin Crane Senior Research Fellow in the Law and Public Affairs Program, Princeton University, and holds the Paul R. Verkuil Chair in Public Law at the Benjamin N. Cardozo School of Law, Yeshiva University. She is the author of the award-winning *God vs. the Gavel: Religion and the Rule of Law* (Cambridge University Press 2005). Hamilton is a former clerk to Justice Sandra Day O'Connor and is also a columnist on constitutional issues for www.FindLaw.com.

*I dedicate this book to the millions of survivors of childhood sexual abuse, who deserve their day in court.*

*I also dedicate it to my wonderful husband,*
*Peter Kuzma, our two terrific children,*
*Will and Alexandra, and my mother, GrandCarol.*
*Thanks for your love, patience, and support!*

# Justice Denied

## What America Must Do to Protect Its Children

**MARCI A. HAMILTON**

Princeton University

CAMBRIDGE
UNIVERSITY PRESS

CAMBRIDGE UNIVERSITY PRESS
Cambridge, New York, Melbourne, Madrid, Cape Town, Singapore, São Paulo, Delhi

Cambridge University Press
32 Avenue of the Americas, New York, NY 10013-2473, USA

www.cambridge.org
Information on this title: www.cambridge.org/9780521886215

First published 2008

Printed in the United States of America

*A catalog record for this publication is available from the British Library.*

*Library of Congress Cataloging in Publication Data*

Hamilton, Marci.
Justice denied : what America must do to protect its children / Marci A. Hamilton.
   p.  cm.
Includes bibliographical references and index.
ISBN 978-0-521-88621-5 (hardback)
1. Child sexual abuse – United States.   2. Child abuse – Law and legislation –
United States.   3. Time (Law) – United States.   I. Title.
KF9323.H36   2008
345.73′025554 – dc22                           2007046278

ISBN 978-0-521-88621-5 hardback

# Contents

# Contents

# Acknowledgments

I sincerely and deeply thank my editor at Cambridge University Press, John Berger, for his insightful support and guidance; Melissanne Scheld at Cambridge for her unflagging efforts to get my ideas to the public; and Liza Murphy for her enthusiastic support of my ideas. I will be forever indebted to Cambridge.

I also owe a sizable debt of gratitude to my phenomenal team of research assistants at Cardozo School of Law, Yeshiva University, including Katie Melvin, Ben Steele, Claire Scheinbaum, Chava Brandriss, Keegan Staker, Elizabeth Pitman, Vikki Elman, Jared Newman, Michelle Haddad, Jason Levy, and Jennifer Blecher. Thanks for your very hard work.

## Acknowledgments

Finally, thanks to Kerry Ledbetter for her great eye and editing.

Princeton University
Fall 2007

# 1

## We Have Failed Our Children

I received an e-mail from an incest survivor that beautifully and tragically captures the rotten core of the legal system's handling of childhood sexual abuse:

> I am a child of sexual abuse at the hands of my father from the age of 6–12 years. He has also abused two other girls that I know of (have proof) one being a friend of mine from school and the other, our babysitter from when I was about 9 years old. I live day to day with the knowledge of these horrors and seem to get tougher day by day with the injustice of seeing nothing being done. Anyway, I called my father 4 years ago and told him that I have somehow found the self esteem and strength to now confront him and make him answer for all the horror he put myself and these two girls (children at the time) through. He basically laughed

at me and told me that there are "Statu[t]e of Limitations."
I pursued the right channels by filing a police report, called
the DA's office, contacted attorneys to see if I could pursue
this, and come to find out he was right.[1]

This survivor had suffered all of those years, but her father
was smugly confident that the law could not make him
accountable for what he had done to her – because of a legal
technicality called the "statute of limitations" (SOL). He was
right.

She was a victim of an arbitrary and technical legal rule
that is keeping survivors like her from getting justice in
almost every state. SOLs are judicial housekeeping rules:
They determine how much time someone has to file a lawsuit
(or a prosecutor has to initiate prosecution). Yes, they are a
boring part of the legal universe, but they are exerting a
cruel force throughout our society, because as the law now
stands in most states, they are set to favor the child predator
and shut out the sexual abuse survivor.

## The Statutes of Limitation Are Arbitrary Technicalities that Routinely Protect Child Sex Abusers from Justice

SOLs are simply the deadlines set by state legislatures and
courts for going to court. A litigant must file her lawsuit
and a prosecutor file charges before the SOL expires. If the
deadline is missed, the litigant or prosecutor is out of luck –
it's just too late to go to court. The SOLs are arbitrary rules,

and they stop litigants even when survivors have strong and just claims.

SOLs can serve good ends. They encourage litigants to get to court before evidence is lost or stale. A good example is the relatively short SOLs covering contract and property disputes. Everyone benefits from a system in which owner-ship of property or products is as clear as possible. These SOLs operate to make sure there is some certainty about who owns what.

At the other end of the spectrum, SOLs can be an unfair and unacceptable barrier to justice. Murder has no SOL because of the heinous nature of the crime, the fact that the victim himself will never be able to bring his cause to justice, and society's interest in identifying murderers.

The central proposition of this book is that the SOL for childhood sexual abuse should be treated like an SOL for murder, not property. Many survivors experience such abuse as the murder of their childhood or their soul. They have an inherently difficult time coming forward, and it is in society's interest to have sex abuse survivors identify child preda-tors for the public in judicial proceedings. Childhood sexual abuse needs to be added to the list of laws that should not be subject to SOLs, and there is a growing grassroots move-ment in the United States to eliminate them.

This is a "how-to" book on stopping child sex abuse, empowering survivors, and helping society identify child predators. The good news is that the answer is straight-forward and attainable: eliminate the SOLs.

*Child sex abuse is a massive national problem: at least*
*25 percent of girls and 20 percent of boys are sexually abused*
The next time you are sitting in a theater, on a bus, strolling through the mall, or anywhere near a group of people, look around: according to the existing studies, at least one in four of the women have been sexually abused as a child, and one in five of the men.[2] In a theater with sixty women and sixty men, that means fifteen of the women and twelve of the men likely were sexually abused. Most of them never told a soul.

Ninety percent of the time, the public does not learn about the abuse, because the survivor does not go to the authorities.[3] As you scan the crowd before you, it is guaranteed that at least one person in the crowd is a sex abuse survivor who has not yet come forward. If given enough time and the right circumstances, though, they will.

I testified before the Delaware Senate in April 2007 in favor of the sort of legislation this book supports. As part of my testimony, I recited the very statistics that you have just read, and then said that I knew there were those in the room who had not yet been able to tell their story. They were the reason I was promoting a change in the law. Then something extraordinary happened: during his remarks in support of this bill, State Sen. John Still (R-Dover North) announced for the first time in his life that a family "friend" sexually abused him when he was six years old. He said, "I have forgiven that person, but I have not forgotten."[4] Everyone in the room was humbled by his modest declaration and reminded that it can take decades, even for the leaders among us, to make such a public declaration.

There are two levels of knowledge about child abuse in the United States. For the majority, childhood sexual abuse is a remote and unlikely event, in part because it never happened to them. Then there is the underground level where the survivors exist, continually adjusting to a world that does not readily acknowledge a permanent part of their identity. The effects of this underworld, though, are felt by all. Whether or not you are a survivor of childhood sexual abuse, you are paying a price in the lost output of the survivors and the mammoth medical costs of treating the physical and psychological injuries of those who have been abused and who may be trying to climb out of the dark.

## The Problem Is Much Closer to Home Than the Old-Fashioned "Stranger Danger" Mythology Would Lead Us to Believe

There was a time when child abusers were referred to as "Stranger Danger." Most of us lived in an unfortunately mythical world where "incest" was only a word in the dictionary, and sexual perverts were just rumors: lurking strangers in trench coats, but not "nice" dads, teachers, or priests. To stay safe, eight-year-old Sally simply had to refuse candy or car rides from "Mr. Stranger Danger." In reality, though, Sally is most at risk from those who care for her and make friends with her, from parents to the chatroom buddy who is in fact a predator.

The busy universe of abuse – for those who are not survivors – has hovered on the bare edges of our vision, like a buzzing bee circling a flower ten feet away; once in a while, you might wonder about Sally's dad because he made you oddly uncomfortable, but the notion that he was raping her in her own bed never came into focus. She did not say anything, even to you, her best friend, because he told her it was "their little secret," and, equally important, because she could not survive without her family. Even more fundamentally, she could not comprehend that he was stealing away the childhood her luckier friends were enjoying. It takes adulthood finally to understand just how much the abuser has taken.

### We are just now piecing together the "big picture" about child abuse

Whether or not one is part of that world of abuse, the wrongheaded way our legal system handles abuse has not been readily apparent. Even if Sally's story seeped out, it would have been regarded as the solitary account of one tragic little girl. The perpetrator was just one man, and so there was no reason to think there was a problem in the system as a whole. The abuser might go to jail, be condemned (or, sadly, protected) by his family, or be shunned by the community, but in the eyes of the public, this one bad man hardly represented a problem that demanded dramatic legal reform.

Only 10 percent of all abuse survivors have come forward to the authorities, and even then, only a tiny number of their stories appear in the news. That means that until very recently, the public would read each story as an isolated, extraordinary situation. The way the data appeared – randomly and shockingly – made it virtually impossible to connect the dots in a way that would expose the system's defects. The inability of the public to piece the story together led survivors to feel chronic isolation; they often believed they were the only ones suffering such horrible nightmares. Perpetrators could abuse victims who were siblings, without either one suspecting the other was equally at risk.

It took orchestrated abuse within a large and venerated institution like the Roman Catholic Church to reveal the depth of the problem to the public in a clear and forceful manner. Let's face it: none of us was looking to learn that child sex abuse is more prevalent than we ever dreamed or that we may not be able to trust – of all people – our neighborhood priest. The shocking but riveting news that the Catholic hierarchy callously shuffled predatory priests from one unsuspecting parish to another finally created an opportunity for the country to begin to see the bare outlines of a society-wide challenge.

The sensational details of the Boston Archdiocese's and Cardinal Bernard Law's handling of infamous former priests John Geoghan and Paul Shanley had to be absorbed before the public could start thinking about the overarching systemic problems. While priests, Geoghan abused more than

130 children,[5] and Shanley advocated quite openly the virtues of the National American Man-Boy Love Association.[6] Geoghan spent his years being moved around the Boston Archdiocese abusing child after child, which led some to believe it was just a local problem.[7] In contrast, Shanley's case provided some of the earliest clues that we had a national problem on our hands: he was transferred from the East Coast to the West Coast where he continued his previous perverted practices.[8] Once these unthinkable facts sunk in, it was inevitable for many to ask what was wrong with the system that produced them.

*Even with the data in place, it can still be tempting to believe that child sex abuse is not as serious a national challenge as it is*

The drive to treat abuse as an idiosyncratic problem that is not a systemic social failure has been strong. Some, like former Sen. Rick Santorum (R-PA), declared that Boston Cardinal Bernard Law's actions were peculiar to Boston, because "[w]hile it is no excuse for this scandal, it is no surprise that Boston, a seat of academic, political and cultural liberalism in America, lies at the center of the storm."[9]

Such reasoning was proven completely wrong when the Philadelphia Grand Jury Report on the Philadelphia Archdiocese was released on Sept. 21, 2005.[10] The report was 423 pages, painfully explicit, and made absolutely clear that Boston's particular moral culture was not responsible for the prevalence of clergy abuse. The Philadelphia Archdiocese's clergy abuse issues were just as foul and prevalent.[11] At the same time that the Philadelphia District Attorney was doggedly investigating the Philadelphia Archdiocese, the Los Angeles District Attorney was vigorously pursuing known abusers, as a California law encouraged hundreds of survivors to come forward. Eventually, we all knew: Abuse within the Church was and is a coast-to-coast phenomenon. Moreover, as the *New York Times* reinforced, abuse is not a problem limited to priests within the institution; it has extended to youth ministers, volunteers, and choir directors as well.[12]

### *The abusers are almost always someone the family knows, who have gained the trust of the victim*

Most perpetrators, like priests, know the victim and the family. Affection, admiration, and trust are typically a vital part of the complex relationship between a child and an abuser well before the sexual abuse even starts. These deceptively "nice guys" and women are usually beloved and trusted members of their schools, churches, or communities, and they "groom" their victims patiently until they can trap the child into sex and silence. Ice cream, outings to the movies, weekend trips to the seashore, and affectionate hugs are all part of this deceptively pleasant predator's ammunition. Often, they will choose a child in an unstable and insecure emotional state; for example, following the death of a parent or a divorce. But this is not always the case: even children in stable conditions with loving families are at risk.

Well over half of all survivors are abused by someone they know – studies indicate that 80 percent of girl survivors, and 60 percent of boy survivors are abused by someone with whom the children have some connection, including relatives, family friends, clergy, teachers, and health care professionals.[13] Shrewd predators seeking children for sex (beyond the cases of incest, where accessibility and power are extraordinary) calculatingly choose careers that will afford them a combination of the greatest access to children and a position that will invite blind trust: teachers, clergy, and day care providers.[14] In the contemporary era, they may also choose online identities that are comfortable and inviting to the child. Far from being "Mr. Stranger Danger," these online predators bank on the same tactics of the predator who is physically present by grooming the child to trust and then obey.

### *Our whole society let down survivors of childhood sexual abuse*
Until recently, the experience of abuse by trusted adults was like a wild ocean storm, where children were violently rocked in sinking ships with life rafts more likely to sink than float. This left some victims to tread water as hard as they could just to stay afloat, while others would sink into suicide or drug or alcohol addiction, not to mention underperformance at work, sexual dysfunction, and difficulties with intimacy that lead to divorce and family disintegration. As children enthralled in relationships with a scheming adult, they simply could not save themselves. Typically, parents let them

down, as did law enforcement, the press, churches, legislatures, and the law.[15]

Too often, parents could not and did not fathom what was happening with their children, even when told. Forceful and sustained denial was the order of the day.[16] When one of Father Raymond Leneweaver's preadolescent survivors told his parents that Leneweaver, of the Philadelphia Archdiocese, had molested him, his father responded by beating him unconscious while repeatedly saying, "[p]riests don't do that."[17]

The press rarely covered child sex abuse, especially when editors were motivated by pressure to protect the reputation of the Church. It was not uncommon for authority figures, like Roman Catholic bishops, to persuade newspaper editors to let them "clean their own dirty laundry." Reporters were fired or moved to other stories after submitting articles to their editors, because the editors believed the material too harsh on the Church.[18] For example, in Milwaukee, Marie Rohde covered the archdiocese even before the *Boston Globe's* pioneering story appeared, and she seemed to be moving toward breaking the predator priest story, but then she found herself re-assigned:

[Rohde] was pulled from the beat in early 1995 by then *Milwaukee Journal* editor Mary Jo Meisner. As a Pressroom column by *Milwaukee Magazine* reported, the archbishop at the time, Rembert Weakland, put pressure on the editors to remove Rohde from the beat.

Seven years later, the *Boston Globe* did its path-breaking series on abusive clergy in America's Catholic Church. The series forced the *Journal Sentinel* to jump belatedly on the issue, but it was not Rohde who was given the assignment.

In retrospect, you can't help wondering what would have happened if Rohde, who can be a very dogged reporter, had been left to dig for dirt on the archdiocese. Perhaps her newspaper, rather than the *Globe*, would have gotten all the glory for this scoop.[19]

Another supposedly safe haven for children – religious organizations – also failed to protect children from abuse, and legislators provided few if any incentives for them to alter their ways. When church lobbyists approached state legislators and asked to be exempt from state law commands to report child abuse, most legislators did not ask the hard question: Why would a religious institution want to keep child abuse a secret? Instead, too many states permitted clergy to avoid reporting known child abuse.

### Widespread childhood sexual abuse always has been there

The reality of massive childhood sexual abuse has always been there – even if it was silent and invisible to most of us. As we have come to learn, the Roman Catholic Church has struggled (unsuccessfully) for centuries to rid itself of clergy abuse of children.[20] The threat to children, therefore, cannot be shrugged off as a random occurrence of current events; rather, abuse has been an entrenched element of the Catholic Church's long history. Plus, the more we have learned about the Church's problems, the more we have come to recognize the abuse within other religious communities, public schools, organizations like the Boy Scouts, and, finally, the home. This enormous problem is rooted in society's attitudes and the law, not just the actions of any one institution at any particular moment.

American society at this time is programmed not to see the abuse, in part because it is done to children, whose political power is insignificant. It will take more than reform of a few private institutions to ensure children are protected – a lot more. Attitudes toward children must change, and the public policy calculus must be tipped in their favor.

### The failures of the legal system are shameful

If 90 percent of child sex abuse is never reported to authorities, a predator may be living next door to you right now – or in your house – and there are few means to be certain about his or her history or propensities. The legal system has made it easy for perpetrators to move from child to child, and state to state, with confidence that they will not be punished for the horrors inflicted on the last child. One crucially important legal reason lies in the inadequate SOLs.

That is why these arbitrary and unjust SOLs must be abolished.

# 2

## What Is Wrong with the System?

### The Courthouse Doors Are Closed to Survivors

The law has been structured so that child predators rarely have to face the legal system for their despicable acts. Justice has been difficult for child sex abuse survivors to obtain because the courthouse doors have been padlocked before they arrived. For decades, the states organized their legal systems in a way that almost always favored the perpetrator by keeping the survivor out of court. When a survivor was finally ready and tapped on the courthouse door, there was no answer, so the survivor quietly retreated. Forget getting survivors' claims before a jury – actions filed by the few brave souls who came forward were usually blocked from the very start by the statutes of limitations (SOLs). Sitting silently behind those few who tried to find justice, but could not, were the millions who never came forward. There were no incentives to draw victims to the courts.

It was not uncommon twenty years ago for states to impose a mere two-year SOL on legal actions concerning childhood sexual abuse, which meant that a child abused at age seven would have to get to court by age nine or else lose the right to sue. There was a lot to lose, including justice and public vindication. If the courts were available, survivors would have two paths to justice and vindication – criminal prosecution and civil actions. Both forums validate the survivor and get the truth to the public. The difference is the remedy: Criminal conviction can put the predator behind bars, while a civil verdict can help the survivor bear the financial cost of the abuse, including therapy and addiction treatment.

The manifest injustice of expecting a survivor of incest or other sex abuse to appear in court while still a child has been felt in the state legislatures, many of which have incrementally and slowly extended the child sex abuse SOL. Over the years, some states have started counting from the age of eighteen, instead of the date of the abuse, and some have added two, five, fifteen, or even twenty-five years to the original SOL. As of 2007, though, only a few did not impose an SOL on the prosecution of a child predator.[1]

To get around the unfair SOLs, some state courts (and some legislatures) devised the "discovery rule": A survivor would not be required to go to court until she understood that her many problems in life were caused by abuse in the past.[2] In other words, she was given time to discover the causal link between the childhood trauma of sexual abuse and her later difficulties. The SOL would be tolled (or stop running) until she had discovered the link between injury and suffering.

For example, a graduate student struggling with alcoholism would not have to go to court until she understood that her addiction arose from the abuse she suffered as a child, or an adult unable to hold down a job would not have to go to court until he learned that the trauma of childhood abuse led to his underperformance at work. As of 1997, more than half of the states recognized a discovery rule for child sex abuse cases.[3]

The discovery rule propped open the courthouse doors for some but still left many survivors facing locked doors, because the time for bringing a lawsuit following discovery was still too short, or the rules for what counted as "discovery" were overly strict. For example, a survivor might have only a year or two following discovery to get a lawyer and get into court.

The system works most often against the best interests of the survivors. While more than half of the states instituted a discovery rule, some still capped the age at which the survivor could file a claim at age eighteen plus two or a few more years, well before most survivors are capable of making their abuse public.[4]

## Childhood Sexual Abuse Survivors Simply Do Not Understand the Harm That Was Done to Them or the Extent of That Harm and So They Do Not Come Forward, Let Alone Go to Court, for Decades

The real problem here is that children who are sexually abused cannot comprehend what is happening to them. Children don't understand what a "childhood" is. How can you know whether someone took away your childhood until you are old enough to know that other people's childhoods were so very different? The short answer is that you cannot. The concept of a "childhood" does not exist for a child. When you are a child, what is "normal" is whatever is happening to you – even when it is truly abnormal.

With regard to sex abuse, the problem is amplified because children do not understand what sex is. Until a child reaches puberty and some understanding of sexuality emerges, an abused young child might sense something is wrong but cannot understand that what happened is, in fact, "sex." Nor can he or she fully comprehend just how monstrous the experience was. They likely feel shame and horror but not because they can intellectually or spiritually assess the crime for what it is. The reality is that it often takes *decades* for a child sex abuse survivor to come forward to family, friends, a spouse, or the authorities.[5]

## There Has Been a Mismatch Between the Ability of Survivors to Come Forward and the Speed With Which the States Expected Them to Do So

Across the country, there has been a fundamental mismatch between the SOLs on child abuse, which cut off claims very quickly, and the ability of children to come forward. Sadly, this situation has created perfect opportunities for predators. Typically, each survivor's right to sue has expired relatively soon after the abuse, meaning that a predator could bank on the likelihood that each new survivor would not be able to get to court. It is eerie how the law dovetailed with the pedophile's predilection for children of a certain age. When the pedophile's interest would wane because the child became too "mature," the ability of the child to go to court would recede well before the child could alert others to the molester's identity. In this topsy-turvy universe, the predator could move on with confidence, knowing the damaged victim was highly unlikely to gain access to the courts, and, therefore, the predator could molest more children under cover. The justice system has been weighted heavily in favor of the adult sexual abuser, whereas it has done little to vindicate the rights of the victim of one of the most heinous crimes.

It defies logic that this legal phenomenon was merely accidental. With the volume of abuse in this country, and with adults' control of the legislative process, survivors' interests simply were not part of any public calculus, whereas the perpetrators' interests were. To be blunt, adults have counted more than children. There has been an exaggerated fear that an adult's reputation would be destroyed by a wrongful accusation, but false accusations have occurred in only a tiny number of cases; procedural safeguards to combat false allegations are already in place.[6]

The perpetrators have had the upper hand during the time they abused the vulnerable child; afterward, they have reaped the benefit of short SOLs.

Only recently have children had a meaningful voice in the legislative process – children were property until not too long ago, and it is my view that it has taken the introduction of more women (and, therefore, mothers) in the legislatures to put children's issues nearer the top of the agenda. It is still too easy for a legislature to sweep children's interests away in the rush of "more pressing" concerns. The diligence of national figures like Oprah Winfrey and John Walsh has been necessary to get children's sex abuse issues somewhere on legislative radar screens. Even so, the legal system usually works for the predator and against the survivor (and the rest of us) – because of the arbitrary SOLs that keep the courthouse doors locked.

# 3

## The Solution Is Clear and Simple

### Abolish the Statutes of Limitation for Childhood Sexual Abuse

Plenty of issues need legislative repair, but many need extensive study before the law is changed. Reform to aid child sex abuse victims does not require this sort of deliberation and delay. The problem is clear and the remedy is simple: get rid of the statutes of limitations (SOLs).

In this chapter, I will explain why this is the obvious and best reform available. Despite the simple logic behind eliminating the SOLs, there has been vigorous, if not desperate, opposition to this sort of reform. In the second half of the book, I will identify who – the insurance industry, the Catholic Church hierarchy, defense attorneys, and teachers – has tried to block legislative change so obviously beneficial for children and our society and why they are opposed. The enemies of reform have fought hard and dirty, but they are losing ground.

## The Vicious Cycle: Survivors Can't Tell, Claims Expire, and Perpetrators Confidently Move On

The law generates a vicious cycle that keeps predators free as it creates more victims. First, survivors of childhood sexual abuse typically take decades to come forward, so even seemingly generous SOLs can be ineffective. Once a survivor's claim is foreclosed, the perpetrator can put another notch on his belt for yet another victim who will be unable to stop his preying behavior.

Second, because of the way we have constructed the system, child sex abuse survivors do not receive adequate encouragement, protection, and nurturing to come forward publicly at all. Only a tiny percentage of childhood sexual abuse survivors ever come to authorities – on the order of about 10 percent. Since the few who do may take decades, we have constructed a comfortable cocoon for the devious perpetrator. No wonder there are so many out there yet to be caught.

These two factors work in synergy to create the reality that survivors are ignored, and we are ignorant about who is a perpetrator and who is not. If you cannot know the identities of the abusing population out there, because they have not been named publicly by survivors, your next-door neighbor, new husband, or child's doctor easily could be a serial child predator. The courthouse doors need to swing open to survivors for the good of all.

## Most Child Abuse Reforms to Date Presume That We Know Who the Predators Are

The United States has tried to curb childhood sexual abuse and violence, but the most popular proposals are largely ineffective because those reforms do not overcome the SOL. States have instituted harsher penalties, including civil commitment,[1] local governments have created "pedophile-free zones" where known pedophiles are not permitted to live,[2] and numerous states have established "Megan's Law" lists that provide the public with names of convicted sex offenders, among other approaches.[3] Each and every one of these reforms presupposes that you know who the child predators are. If you do not, you simply cannot put him in jail longer, keep him out of your "pedophile-free zone," or place him on a registered sex offender list.

**Harsher penalties.** Sentences for sex offenders have expanded dramatically in a number of states, with even the death penalty as an option for some prosecutors. In 2005, Florida enacted Jessica's Law, named after Jessica Lunsford, a nine-year-old who was abducted and murdered by a known sex offender with a history of crimes against children. The law requires lifetime monitoring by a Global Positioning Satellite (GPS) of certain sex offenders, enforces the sex offender registration requirement, and criminalizes the act of harboring a sex offender in violation of the duty to register.

Moreover, the law imposes a mandatory twenty-years-to-life sentence for many offenders whose victims are children.[4] Connecticut took up the issue in 2007 as well, passing a twenty-five-year sentence for the first conviction on aggravated sexual assault against a child under thirteen and then a mandatory fifty-year sentence for a second offense.[5]

In 2006, South Carolina enacted a law allowing the death penalty for sex offenders if the accused was twice convicted of raping a child younger than eleven years old.[6] The same year, Oklahoma Gov. Brad Henry followed South Carolina's example, signing a law making those found guilty of repeated rape or other sex crimes against children younger than fourteen eligible for the death penalty,[7] while Texas Gov. Rick Perry signed such a bill in July 2007.[8] Louisiana law also permits prosecutors to seek the death penalty for the rape of children younger than twelve.[9]

**Civil commitment.** States have tried to keep predators off the streets through a variety of means, both civil and criminal. In 1996, the U.S. Supreme Court upheld the practice of committing a sexually violent predator to a civil institution following a prison sentence, because if the predator's crimes were due to "a mental abnormality or a personality disorder," the person is likely to commit another violent crime.[10] The New York courts, countering the trend in other states, recently limited involuntary commitment of prison inmates to psychiatric hospitals despite vigorous resistance by Gov. Pataki, who was intent on keeping sex offenders off the streets.[11] Pataki unilaterally ordered men deemed dangerous sex offenders be held following release from prison; he took the action out of frustration with the state assembly's refusal to pass a bill allowing involuntary civil confinement of sex offenders.[12] The New York courts did not side with Pataki. In a unanimous decision, the New York State Court of Appeals, agreeing with a lower court finding, ruled that a hearing must be held to determine whether the inmate should remain in custody.[13] While I favor finding ways to keep perpetrators away from children, this is another reform that rests on the assumption that we know who the perpetrators are.

**Tracking.** GPS tracking of sexual predators has been instituted as well. In 2007, North Carolina was considering a bill that would require sex offenders to be registered before release from prison and tracked by GPS linked to ankle bracelets. The duration of the tracking would vary, depending on the conviction, with repeat offenders and those convicted of aggravated assault monitored for life.[14] As of mid-2007, approximately twenty-eight states had passed legislation employing some form of electronic tracking of sex offenders.[15]

**Pedophile-free zones.** There is a natural instinct to try to keep anything injurious to children away from them. For example, many localities have laws that forbid adult entertainment and liquor stores from locating near schools, churches, and residential neighborhoods. The same principle of physical distance is being applied to pedophiles, creating what are called "pedophile-free zones." For example, in Hamilton Township, New Jersey, no convicted child sex offender may live within 2,500 feet of schools, parks, or playgrounds.[16]

Unfortunately, this approach has a lot more surface appeal than practical effect. It is a license to a false sense of security for parents. As I commented in my FindLaw.com column of Aug. 25, 2005, "[e]ven if a pervert cannot live within 2,500 feet of a school, he will doubtless be able (either legally, or due to the limits of enforcement) to use the sidewalks and streets near schools and playgrounds... they prey on children wherever they can find them, not just at school or at the playground. And no zoning program will ever be able to address that risk."[17] Again, this type of law rests on the assumption that predators are already identified. It does nothing to expand the category of known predators.

**Megan's Law.** States now maintain lists of convicted sex offenders to inform the public of their presence. This tactic is undermined by overly short criminal SOLs. If a predator is never prosecuted because the SOL closed before the victim could get to court, there is no conviction, and, therefore, there is no name to add to the public list. The Supreme Court held in *Stogner v. California* that once a criminal SOL runs out on particular criminal acts, a victim may not file charges against the defendant without violating the Ex Post Facto Clause. The result is that the Megan's Law lists in the states will be inadequate to fully alert the public about predators for decades to come.

## Mandatory Child Abuse Reporting Is Inadequate by Itself

Child abuse reporting requirements and mandatory background checks have expanded.[18] But with its naive attitude toward religion, the United States has been especially slow to require religious entities to report suspected abuse. For example, while Colorado's list of mandatory reporters has grown since it was reenacted in 1987, clergy members were not added as reporters until 2002. The list now includes clergy where they belong – in a long list of those with access to children, including health care professionals and personnel engaged in the admission, care, or treatment of patients; Christian Science practitioners; public or private school officials or employees; social workers; mental health professionals; veterinarians; peace officers; pharmacists; commercial film and photographic print processors; firefighters; victims' advocates; licensed marriage and family therapists; juvenile parole and probation officers; child and family investigators; officers and agents of the state bureau of animal protection; and animal control officers.[19]

It is true that reporting can increase our data bank of known predators, but experience shows that unless the penalties for failure to report are stiff (e.g., prison time or high fines), many institutions and individuals ignore the reporting laws. In most states, failure to report is at best a misdemeanor accompanied by small fines. In addition, such reports too often get lost in the state bureaucracies.

Most of the policies mentioned above are defensible, but none adequately increases our knowledge of the predators' identities as long as SOLs are shutting out many survivors before they can get to the courthouse. The legal system has disabled the single most important source of information about predators – the survivors themselves – by imposing unreasonable SOLs.

The SOLs are a dam holding back the identities of predators from the public. The only way to enrich the databank of predator identities and to provide survivors with vindication and justice is to give those survivors more time, indeed, all the time they need, to prosecute and to file civil lawsuits.

If the SOLs are abolished, each one of these legislative strategies becomes a more effective tool to reduce the incidence of child sex abuse. We would have more perpetrators to sentence and place in civil confinement and more information to publish on Megan's Law lists and more names for background checks. Here is the conundrum: you can harshly punish every known predator right up to the edges of the Eighth Amendment's rule against cruel and unusual punishment, but if you are punishing only a handful of the existing predators, children are still in serious peril.

## Compelling Public Interests Support Window Legislation

The following four public policies are achieved when the SOLs are eliminated. They add up to one overarching policy: the safety of children is more important than the comfort of child abusers.

*Public policy #1: accommodating the needs of childhood sex abuse survivors by crafting a system that makes them the priority instead of their predators*

The best means to accommodate the needs of child sex abuse survivors is to be patient: these survivors need to know they will be able to obtain justice at some point, when they are ready, and that no one will judge them for taking the time they need. If the incest survivor needs decades to leave home, free herself financially, and establish her own identity before being able to confront the father who raped her in her childhood bed, then so be it. As a society, we need to send a message that her healing is our foremost concern and that we value her needs far above her perpetrator's desire to have closure on criminal and civil liability.

The answer, then, is to prop open the courthouse door, and leave it open for childhood sexual abuse cases. No artificial deadline should halt the survivor who is finally able to stand on the courthouse steps and tell the world that a horrible crime was done to her or him. There should be no arbitrary and rigid time frame that permits the multimillionaire parent or wealthy institution that fostered the sex abuse to believe their assets are wholly protected from the victims they destroyed. Certainly, no perpetrator or institution that aided that perpetrator should be secure in the knowledge that jail time and fines are beyond the survivor's reach.

In short, empower the survivor with open access to the justice system and, at the same time, introduce tension and fear into the lives of those who caused and permitted the abuse to happen. Without changing anything else in the law, broadly eliminating the SOLs will dramatically shift the balance of power to the survivors.

### Public policy #2: identifying the child predators in our midst

If survivors can file their claims in court and make their experiences public, the rest of us can learn who the hidden predators are. This is the best means available to increase the public's knowledge about the child perpetrators in its midst.

If the legal system is available to the survivor, we all benefit from the public identification of the perpetrator – whenever it occurs. Predators typically prey on children throughout their entire lives, so identifying predators when they are elderly can still prevent future abuse.[20] It is the best public policy to stop them at any point in their careers.

John Geoghan, of the Boston Archdiocese, was not tried and convicted until 2002 at the age of sixty-six, nearly forty years after he began molesting children.[21] He was most recently accused of fondling a boy in 1995 and 1996 as he drove the boy around Boston; at the time, Geoghan was nearly sixty.[22] If survivors are relieved of the SOL and can get to court, they can unmask the perpetrators still grooming children into their elderly years.

### *Public policy #3: finding more survivors of the same perpetrator once a single survivor has come forward*

If survivors can enter the courthouse at any time, there is a bonus when more predators are publicly identified – more survivors come forward.

During 2003 in California, a window was in effect that eliminated all SOLs for survivors for one year, and it was a common experience that once one survivor named a particular perpetrator, other survivors of the same abuser soon followed. Prosecutors were also aided in identifying more survivors. Discovering their fellow survivors led many to feel crushing regret for not having told anyone earlier, because they might have prevented abuse that happened after their own. But, at the same time, finding fellow survivors was also a relief.

The identification of the other survivors of the same perpetrator vindicated them in the public's eye: now the abuse was obviously not their fault; the perpetrator was an evil individual, and any institution that permitted the perpetrator to gain access to them was equally evil. Years of guilt ceded ground to relief and a renewed sense of self. As one survivor who would benefit from Delaware's retroactive abolition of the civil SOL explained, "I never got a chance to see the man who abused me for years when I was a child get punished and yet I live as a punished woman for crimes he committed upon me. My voice was stilled by the old law. My voice has new life now. Thank you for giving my voice life."[23]

This is not to say that coming forward is ever easy for a survivor of childhood sexual abuse, because even when years have passed, the pain is still searing. To one thirty-seven-year-old man, "[f]iling charges was a double-edged sword. While it was gratifying, it also forced [him] to relive his painful past and revisit the emotional trauma he's endured since. [His] burden has lifted somewhat, he said. He has sought counseling and is now able to discuss the incident openly with his wife. But the raw pain is still there."[24]

Just one survivor, though, can make a big difference. Michael Wempe, sixty-six, a retired Roman Catholic priest from the Los Angeles Catholic Archdiocese, was once charged with molesting thirteen boys in the 1970s and 1980s. The case was dismissed, however, because the United States Supreme Court struck down the California law permitting retroactive criminal prosecution of decades-old sex abuse cases. Three months after this ruling, which voided forty-two other sexual abuse allegations against Wempe,[25] another man came forward alleging he had been molested by Wempe in the 1990s and whose claims were within the SOL. Wempe was sentenced to ten years in prison this time, and served three. This survivor's service to society did not end with criminal prosecution and incarceration of a dangerous serial predator. Just identifying his name to the public made it easier to protect kids in the future: After Wempe was paroled, demonstrators picketed his retirement residence in order to alert neighbors that a child predator was nearby.[26] In another case, the Los Angeles District Attorney's Office investigated former priest Michael Baker for alleged child sex abuse and requested Baker's personnel files from the Los Angeles Archdiocese, which fought hard to keep the files secret. After losing all the way up to the Supreme Court, the archdiocese finally was forced to turn over the files and the District Attorney's Office learned of a second alleged victim based on the files alone. But for the investigation of the first alleged victim, the office might never have known about the existence of the second.[27]

There are even cases where siblings or relatives discovered they had been abused by the same predator only after a lawsuit was filed.[28] For example, in early 2006, five brothers and sisters from the same Long Island, New York, family filed a $25 million lawsuit against the Diocese of Rockville Centre claiming that the hierarchy covered up their sexual abuse as children by the same priest. Dick Regan and his siblings alleged abuse by Father Daniel Babis (now deceased) and an orchestrated cover-up by Bishop William Murphy, dating back to the first reports of the abuse in 1968. Regan said he always knew that he and one of his sisters were molested by Babis, starting in the mid-1950s, but only discovered decades later that three other siblings also had been carrying the same terrible secret. He learned that one of his sisters remembers herself and another brother being molested by Babis – a family "friend" who took them on trips and kneeled at their bedside to fondle them.[29]

In the same vein, in January 2002, survivor Michael Vernig called attorney Michael Morey after seeing Morey's name in the press coverage of survivors joining a lawsuit against Thomas Laughlin, a former priest in the Archdiocese of Portland, Oregon, who was convicted of sex abuse in 1983. When Vernig heard that his abuser, Laughlin, had been living on a church pension in a community where no one knew of his past abuse, he was motivated to disclose the secret he had harbored since his childhood. Vernig had no idea that his older brother, Tom, had called Morey only months earlier. By May of that year, the two brothers spoke and realized that they both were abused by the same man when they served as altar boys at All Saints Catholic Church in Northeast Portland over twenty years ago.[30]

Sadly, it is not unusual for a predator to expand from one child within a family to siblings. In January 2006, Father James Harris was accused of sexually abusing six of eight siblings when they were between the ages of five and fourteen, who he came to know after taking up a collection for them following a fire at their home in 1968. Harris was not the only abuser preying on the family: Sometime between 1969 and 1972, Father Maurice Grammond also allegedly abused three of the children when Harris took them to Seaside, Oregon, for a visit to the rectory.[31]

*Public policy #4: deterring institutions from hiding child sex abuse*
Institutions dealing with children must be part of the solution. History shows that institutions need to be coerced to protect the interests of children. The law must change so that business and nonprofit employers find it in their self-interest to turn in child abusers; and they will do that more readily when they know that there will never be a time when their liability and the perpetrator's liability disappears.

Children have been in such an inferior social position that there is hardly an institution that has not consciously (or unconsciously) favored its own interests over the child's. According to the *Philadelphia Daily News*, the Philadelphia Convention Center (PCC) knew that one of its employees, David Morgenstern, acting director of Events Services at the PCC, had made improper use of his computer several years ago. Then, in April 2007, a father complained to PCC President Al Mezzaroba that the same employee was engaging in sexually suggestive chatting online with his fifteen-year-old daughter. Instead of contacting law enforcement, which Mezzaroba said was the duty of the girl's father, Mezzaroba initiated an internal investigation, seized Morgenstern's hard drive, and placed Morganstern on paid "family and medical leave."[32] Despite the obvious potential for criminal culpability, Mezzaroba said "the only allegation is misuse of a computer ... [and o]ur obligation is to make sure an employee didn't do anything improper on our time."[33] The state police rightly asked: Since when does a convention center become the state's investigating arm for potential child abuse? Too often, private or quasi-public entities act as though they must take on the role of the police when all they should do is contact the police.

The convention center story shows how necessary it is to push and prod institutions to act outside their usual frame of reference and to safeguard the best interests of all children. The best and easiest way to accomplish that goal is to increase their incentives to protect children by eliminating the SOLs that have perennially shielded them from accountability for their knowing, reckless, and negligent behavior toward children.

# 4

## What It Will Take to Protect Children

### What the States Must Do; What the Federal Government Should Do

I suppose it comes as no surprise at this point for me to say that the statutes of limitations (SOLs) for childhood sexual abuse need to be abolished across the board. Now that principle must be translated into reality.

#### WHAT THE STATES MUST DO

The laws relating to childhood sexual abuse cover a fair amount of legal territory, with the two main arenas being the private sphere (companies and nonprofit organizations) and the public sphere (public schools and government agencies). My view is that children deserve to be protected wherever they are, and so the SOL for childhood sexual abuse should be abolished in all circumstances.

For the state legislator, though, this task is not quite so simple. The law itself is typically divided between public and private spheres, and therefore these reforms often should be considered separately in each arena. There are distinct issues with respect to each realm, and so the elimination of the SOL needs to be handled in a two-step fashion.

## State Reform in the Private Sphere

Reforming the SOL for childhood sexual abuse in the private sphere is uncomplicated. Two reforms are necessary in order to serve the four public policy goals I detailed in Chapter 3:

(1) Accommodating the needs of childhood sex abuse survivors by crafting a system that makes them and not the predators the priority;
(2) Identifying the child predators in our midst;
(3) Finding more survivors of the same perpetrator once a single survivor has come forward;
(4) Deterring institutions from hiding child sex abuse.

*First, abolish the statutes of limitation going forward*
*for all childhood sexual abuse involving private individuals*
*and organizations*

By abolishing the SOLs for all acts of childhood sexual abuse starting on the date of the law's effect, a state can ensure that no survivor whose SOL has not yet expired will ever be denied a fair hearing. Instead, survivors will have the time they need, and the public will know the names of perpetrators that we never would have obtained if the survivors continued to be barred from the courts. Both criminal prosecution and civil actions should be available to a survivor when that survivor is ready, regardless of the date.

A number of states do not impose an SOL on criminal prosecution relating to child sex abuse. For example, Alabama has no limitation for prosecuting any sexual offense involving a minor under the age of sixteen.[1] A few other states do not have statutes of limitations for categories of felonies, including Florida, Virginia, and Wyoming. A number of other states do not impose a limitation for certain offenses involving child sexual abuse. (See Appendix to Chapter 4.)

At least three states have abolished the SOL for civil claims for damages. The Child Victim's Act of Delaware, which went into effect on July 10, 2007, abolished the civil SOL for childhood sexual abuse. Alaska and Maine abolished their SOLs in 2001 and 1999, respectively. (The legislative language from selected state statutes can be found in the Appendix to Chapter 4.)

There is a second-best option in the civil context. Though not as comprehensive, it also would be a large step in the right direction for survivors. (It is also more complicated.) Instead of clear-cut abolition, as in Delaware, a state could institute a "discovery rule," as it is called. Under this system, which I first mentioned in Chapter 2, a survivor might have a limit on when he or she could go to court, but that limit would be tied to the date the survivor fully realized that his or her personal problems were caused by the sexual abuse as a child. In other words, the SOL would not even start running until the survivor had come to the full realization that his or her dysfunction was triggered by childhood sex abuse. The state could then provide a generous time period following the discovery, say, ten years.

States, including California, Minnesota, and Florida, currently apply codified (in other words, legislative) versions of the discovery rule. The District of Columbia is considering just such a proposal. One advantage of the discovery approach is that the law is tailored to the individual survivor and takes into account the special difficulties sex abuse victims face in coming forward. Like the abolition of the SOL, the discovery rule sends the message that society's priority is the survivor – not the predator.

### Second, create a "window" for sexual abuse survivors whose civil claims were cut short by an overly short SOL in the past

The law governing childhood sexual abuse has been so inadequate for so long, though, that fixing only the SOL going forward is insufficient. The primary problem is that so many perpetrators have been able to sneak under the wire of the SOL, so their identities remain locked outside the halls of justice. The bar to justice must be lifted here, too, which means that an SOL that already expired should be suspended for enough time to permit survivors to file their claims. In other words, the SOL may have ended, but the state legislature can now declare it reopened.

This strategy has been nicknamed the "window" approach, because it creates a window of opportunity for survivors to identify perpetrators and to obtain some measure of justice.

California created both a criminal and a civil window. The former was struck down for constitutional reasons, but the latter has survived such challenges. The California legislature instituted a window for the criminal prosecution of a child predator in 1993 and then for civil actions, such as personal injury claims, in 2003. (Minnesota was actually the first state to try a window, in 1989.)[2] Unfortunately, a closely divided United States Supreme Court, in the summer of 2003, ruled in *Stogner v. California* that opening a window for *criminal* prosecution was unconstitutional.[3] Five members of the court ruled that the Ex Post Facto Clause of the Constitution prohibited reopening a criminal SOL. Thus, once a criminal SOL runs, the criminal justice system cannot be the vehicle for survivors who have neither gone to court to obtain justice nor identified predators to the public.

That means that the *only* legal option to permit survivors – whose claims have already expired – to obtain justice is to open a window for their civil claims. That is exactly what the California legislature did by enacting a law that lifted the SOL for civil claims in childhood sex abuse cases, allowing even decades-old claims to be brought during the

2003 calendar year. As a result, over 1,000 lawsuits were filed by survivors that year and the identities of approximately 300 perpetrators previously unknown to the public were revealed.[4] Delaware passed more generous window legislation in 2007, which runs for two years starting on July 10, 2007.

In order to get as many perpetrators' names to the public as possible, civil windows must be passed in every state. The length of the window is a matter of state legislative choice. California's was one year, Delaware's is two years, and other states have considered five years. If it were up to me, I would simply abolish the SOL in all cases (so that the window would permanently be open), but to date, such an approach does not mesh with political reality, as I will explain in later chapters where I discuss the determined opponents of legislative reform.

## State Reform for State and Local Institutions

The same principles justify abolishing SOLs for childhood sexual abuse that was perpetrated in the public sphere as well. Whether a child is sexually abused by a private school or a public school teacher, the same dynamic operates to slow the survivor's ability to get to court.

The technical, legal question in the public arena is whether sovereign immunity must be removed as well. (Sovereign immunity is the principle that the government cannot be sued by private entities. It is intended to prevent individuals from being enriched to the detriment of other citizens of the sovereign and the common good.) Typically, sovereign immunity protects a state's treasury from private lawsuits in order to shield a state from onerous interference with the performance of its governmental duties and to preserve its control over state property and funds that might otherwise be endangered if the state could be subject to suit by every citizen.[5] Thus, child sex abuse survivors of public entities typically have at least two high hurdles to clear: a short SOL (sometimes a matter of months) and sovereign immunity.

State legislators have an obligation to investigate the financial and legal ramifications of eliminating the SOLs for childhood sexual abuse by state employees. Hearings need to be held and public discussion fostered. In all other areas of state liability, there are potent arguments for an SOL, because the state wants the illegal behavior to be halted as soon as possible and the adults involved are not inherently disabled from bringing the claims. For example, adult employees usually have a relatively short time to file sexual harassment claims against the state. But childhood sexual abuse is different. It is a category that can be distinguished from all others because sex abuse survivors almost always need the time that SOLs deny them. The adult bringing a sexual harassment claim is in a different position from the child sex abuse survivor, who labors under a built-in dynamic that frequently slows the sex abuse survivor's movement toward the justice system.

States, just like private institutions, need to be deterred by law from covering up the identities of abusers and be held publicly accountable by survivors. If the SOLs are eliminated in the state sphere, there is a powerful motive to identify predators and remove them. That motive is criminal and civil liability.

Typically, as in Delaware, the state will need to allocate some funds to buy insurance or designate an amount for self-insurance to cover such cases. It will also have to educate the public on why the public good demands the elimination of the SOL going forward and through window legislation. As I have said before, one of the key elements at stake is protecting future children from abuse by identifying abusers. This goal is just as important in the public realm as in the private. Predators draw no such distinction.

Child predators actively seek careers and vocations that give them access to children, whether the job is public or private. In his widely cited 2001 publication distributed by the National Center for Missing & Exploited Children, former FBI Special Agent Kenneth Lanning noted that "a pedophile may seek employment where he will be in contact with children (e.g., teacher, camp counselor, babysitter, school-bus driver) or where he can eventually specialize in dealing with children (e.g., physician, dentist, clergy member, photographer, social worker, law-enforcement officer)."[6] Predators are devious by nature, and until SOLs stop sheltering them from culpability, they will have the ability to move fluidly between public and private spheres and from child to child.

## WHAT THE FEDERAL GOVERNMENT SHOULD DO

The laws at issue here – criminal and tort laws governing childhood sexual abuse – are usually the states' domain, and so the federal government is not in a position to change these laws by itself. But there are ways for the federal government to encourage the states to enact appropriate SOLs for childhood sexual abuse. (Don't forget that the federal government does have some criminal law governing child abuse, especially when a child is taken across state or national lines.)

There are a number of national interests at stake. First, unidentified child predators move freely across state lines all the time. Each state with a deficient SOL puts the children just over the border at risk, as well as those across the country. Moreover, federal initiatives are undermined by inadequate SOLs. For example, Congress recently passed the Adam Walsh Child Protection and Safety Act, which mandated a national database of registered sex offenders. Like the Megan's Law lists in the various states, the list is far from comprehensive, because we need a better legal system to identify the perpetrators.

Second, there is a huge, though sadly underexamined, economic cost at the national level, caused by the prevalence of childhood sexual abuse. Those who are sexually abused tend to have higher than normal rates of alcohol and drug abuse, mental health issues, sexual dysfunction issues, and suicide rates. Each one of these issues imposes large health care costs, some of which have to be covered by federal medical funding, especially when the abuser is disabled by the abuse experience, and all of which increase health care costs. Childhood sexual abuse imposes an indirect cost to every American in the form of higher insurance premiums generated by more claims. In addition, many survivors suffer from a loss of productivity in their careers that also depletes the national economy. Thus, Congress rightly should study and consider how it can reduce the incidence of childhood sexual abuse, which is generating this heavy economic burden.

An obvious first step at the national level was already taken: in 2003,[7] Congress abolished the criminal SOL for crimes involving child sexual or physical abuse or the kidnapping of a child under the age of eighteen.[8]

The federal government also needs to find ways to encourage states to eliminate their SOLs. One approach would be for Congress to pass a law that would reward states for abolishing the civil and criminal SOLs – the promise of meaningful funds can be a powerful state motivator. The federal government uses this carrot-and-stick approach regularly, following the landmark decision of *South Dakota v. Dole*, in which the Supreme Court held it constitutional for the federal government to condition the receipt of federal funds on mandated state actions.[9] The federal law challenged (and upheld) in *Dole* withheld a portion of federal highway funds if the state had a minimum drinking age below twenty-one. Similarly, in *Jackson v. Birmingham Board of Education*, the Supreme Court held that Title IX (which prohibits intentional sex discrimination in athletic programs) was enacted under Congress's power to spend for the national welfare, and, therefore, Congress could condition receipt of federal funds to schools on agreement to accept liability for discrimination.[10]

Here, Congress and the president could promise to increase by a certain percentage the usual federal funds allocated for health care or law enforcement involving sex offenders, child protective services, or other related programs if the states abolish the criminal and civil SOL and create a civil window. Congress could also use the prod of threatening to withdraw a percentage of pre-existing federal funds if the state fails to enact SOL reform.

Naysayers will say that child abuse is a state issue, but it is far too late to say that the federal government is not involved in the prevention and reduction of child sex abuse. To the contrary, as the following examples attest, it is already in a position where it can use its clout to guide the states toward a set of policies that are friendly to child sex abuse survivors.

Such funding is not uncommon. For example, the Adam Walsh Child Protection and Safety Act of 2006 provides federal grants to combat child sexual abuse, including Project Safe Childhood, which provides federal funds for the integration of federal, state, and local efforts to investigate and prosecute cases of child exploitation.[11] The act also funds law enforcement training, investigation, and community education and outreach;[12] the establishment and maintenance of education programs for children and parents on Internet safety by states, local governments, and nonprofit organizations;[13] and the Rape, Abuse & Incest National Network (RAINN), which operates free and confidential survivors' telephone and online hotlines as well as rape crisis centers.[14] Federal funds also have been allocated for child abuse–related issues in many other areas, including to the provision of in-home health services to abused or neglected children;[15] to public and nonprofit private entities to provide services to children of substance abusers;[16] to state child and family services programs to prevent the neglect, abuse, or exploitation of children;[17] to state courts assessing foster care and adoption to ensure the safety of children and collaboration with child services to track and analyze child abuse and neglect cases;[18] to programs for mentoring the children of prisoners among whom problems of child abuse and neglect exist;[19] to community-based efforts to prevent and treat child abuse and neglect as well as provision of family support services;[20] to states for the development of safe havens for children during child parent visitation to reduce the incidence of child abuse or sexual assault;[21] to states' crime victims assistance programs, including victims of child abuse and sexual assault;[22] and to nonprofit public or private entities providing enforcement assistance for child abuse, sexual assault, and related issues in rural communities.[23] Without a doubt, there is enough federal involvement in this arena to date to set the stage for Congress to create incentives for the states to eliminate their SOLs governing childhood sexual abuse.

There is no question that the laws need to change at the state level, and the federal government has more than sufficient justification to prod them toward the goals of increased public knowledge and greater justice.

### It will take the whole country to turn the tide in favor of child sex abuse survivors

They say it takes a village to raise a child. In fact, it will take concerted effort on the part of the entire country to protect our children from sexual abuse. Right now, we have the icing on the cake with longer sentences, Megan's Laws, and other mechanisms that apply to identified predators. The problem is that we do not have the cake itself: we need the law to do a much better job of identifying perpetrators in the first place. We need the survivors to be able to go to court and publicly name their predators.

The solution is to abolish the SOLs, backward and forward, and the most effective route to that end is to enlist both the state and federal governments.

# 5

## Barrier #1

### The Insurance Industry

No matter the issue, it is wise to follow the trail of money to understand what is really happening. When the issue is legal reform to benefit childhood sexual abuse survivors, the trail has often ended at the insurance industry. Although the hierarchy of the Roman Catholic Church has been the most publicly active entity to battle such reform to date, the insurance lobbyists have been the quieter and more deadly opposition. To date, they have worked in tandem.

Many will say, understandably, "Wait a minute, what the heck does the insurance industry have to do with child abuse?" One outraged blogger commenting on the Los Angeles Archdiocese's $660 million settlement with clergy abuse survivors in 2007 put it like this:

(1) The key words [in the news coverage], for me, are *insurance* and, then, *sexual abuse insurance*. The Catholic Church in LA has ... sexual abuse insurance. *Sexual abuse insurance.*

(2) This is wrong on so many different levels ... but after grappling with it, I came down to two things that really bake my noodle. The first is that *you can buy sexual abuse insurance*. The second is that *someone actually bought sexual abuse insurance*.

(3) This is just killing me. That there are companies – no, no, companies do nothing, there are *people* who said, "Oh, yeah, we're willing to give you liability coverage in case someone in your institution rapes children. We're comfortable making a profit off of helping your institution protect itself from punishments you'd get from systematic child abuse on a monstrous scale and your morally indefensible cover-ups of these crimes." I mean, even beyond the legality of something like this, the simple *morality* of it ... This *boggles* my mind.

(4) The second part of my near death experience is that the Catholic Church *sought out* this kind of insurance. You only get insurance against events you think might actually happen.[1]

Here is the reality: Religious groups are employers, and all employers need insurance to protect themselves from liability for the bad behavior of their employees. As I explain in *God vs. the Gavel*, we Americans tend to put on rose-colored glasses when it comes to religion. The notion that a revered religious organization like the Roman Catholic Church would have sex abuse insurance may offend our sensibilities. For the sake of our children, though, everyone needs to take off the rose-tinted glasses and understand that religious groups are just like every other group – capable of harm and in need of legal deterrence and insurance.

Without the law and insurance companies shaping corporate behavior, religious groups will err just as often as every other humanly run institution. (I often say that the biggest problem with organized religion is the human factor.) So, yes, churches have had and will continue to need sexual abuse insurance – like every other institution. One of the reasons is that we know the identities of so few of the perpetrators at this point.

Companies like the National Catholic Risk Retention Group (TNCRRG) provide such liability coverage for churches, and actively educate them in defending against survivors. TNCRRG has put together a "child sexual abuse prevention system known as the Protecting God's Children[TM] program . . . [which includes] a series of claim/litigation management workshops . . . [with] defense preparation (including First Amendment issues, statute of limitation issues, discovery considerations, and litigation planning and management protocols, processes, and procedures) . . . [and] networking with other diocesan counsel, deriving support from the USCCB [U.S. Conference of Catholic Bishops], interacting with the district attorney, and accessing appropriate medical and psychological consultation."[2] Make no mistake about it, insurance coverage of religious organizations is big business.

To date, the insurance industry has sided with its organizational consumers and tried to undermine childhood sexual abuse legislative reform, but, as I discuss at the end of this chapter, there is good reason to question whether insurance companies have followed the most profitable business model on these issues. It is not in their interest to keep the identities of predators secret.

## The Insurance Industry Has Worked Hard to Kill Child Sex Abuse Legislative Reform

Denver Bishop Charles J. Chaput succeeded in defeating legislative reform in Colorado through shameless (and expensive) antics, but it is unlikely that he would have been victorious over the survivors of childhood sexual abuse if not for the insurance industry. As the *Rocky Mountain News* reported, the "[insurance] industry . . . turned the tide against the [reform bill]. 'It was giving them heartburn,' said the bill's sponsor, Rep. Gwyn Green, D-Golden."[3]

One would be hard-pressed to find insurance industry spokespersons backing any kind of extended statute of limitation (SOL) for child sex abuse. They issue platitudes about needing "reasonable" laws: "Our industry is interested in a reasonable statute of limitations – without it, it's difficult for businesses to defend themselves," said Robert Ferm, of the American Insurance Association.[4] But behind closed doors (and talking among themselves), they sing quite a different tune, which goes something like, "protect the abusers and their enablers at all costs, because otherwise we'll have to pay." For example, the Insurance Institute of Indiana touted one of its "legislative successes" as "[d]efeating [a] measure that would have extended the statute of limitations for civil actions brought in cases of childhood sexual assault."[5]

### The Insurance Industry Is a Lobbying Power Extraordinaire (Pity the Little Children)

There is hardly a more powerful set of lobbyists in the United States than those laboring for the insurance industry. One can only imagine the disparity in power between children and the insurance companies – child advocates often must explain why children's interests so often fall off the public agenda. They point out, "[c]hildren don't vote." Nor do their advocates have the resources to lobby like the insurance industry. That is why it takes legislators of extraordinary vision to do what is right for children in the United States.

Second only to the pharmaceutical and health products industry, the insurance industry spent over $130 million on lobbying in 2006 and over $890 million from 1998 to 2006.[6] In 2005, insurance, finance, and real estate composed the largest sector of lobbying spending, expending over $340 million.[7] In the state of Washington alone, the insurance lobby spent over $800,000 from January to May 2007.[8] Furthermore, the insurance business represents the largest U.S. industrial market based on the North American Industrial Code System. In 2007, insurance carriers were projected to generate over $1.36 trillion in revenue. In contrast, the next largest U.S. market, automotive manufacturers, were projected to generate $785 billion in revenue.[9]

The result is that insurance lobbyists rarely have to take a public position on an issue if they do not want to, and they have no such desire in the child abuse legislative reform arena. Who would want to take a public position so obviously at odds with the interests of children, families, and child sex abuse survivors? Not even the insurance industry, which has instructed its lobbyists to date to quietly kill SOL reform.

Insurance carriers typically work by stealth because they can. They simply visit elected representatives behind closed doors and voilà! The bill they dislike is dead.[10] That has been true in general for SOL reform. Whereas the press and the public might know about the lobbying by the hierarchy of the Catholic Church, the schoolteachers, and the defense attorneys, the insurance industry's subterranean opposition is usually apparent only by inference. For example, when window legislation was pending in Ohio, the public did not know that insurance industry representatives were hard at work fighting it. Ultimately, though, the industry was given equal billing with the bishops when the window legislation was removed from the bill. The *Dayton Daily News* reported,

> [Ohio] State Sen. Marc Dann, a candidate for Ohio attorney general, said this week he will continue to push for a one-year window that would allow childhood victims of sexual abuse to sue over abuse that occurred as long as 35 years ago . . . That provision was stripped from state legislation last week after intense lobbying by Catholic bishops and insurance companies, angering adult victims of childhood sexual abuse by priests.[11]

### Even before the Clergy Abuse Crisis Hit the Headlines in 2002, the Insurance Companies Were Working against Survivors of Clergy Abuse in Colorado

I first encountered the insurance industry phenomenon in Colorado in 1999 when a "Fiduciary Duty Bill," HB 99-1260, was introduced in the Colorado legislature, which would have immunized religious organizations from liability for sexually abusing clergy. Hardly anyone understood from the vanilla language of the bill that it was aimed at protecting church coffers, though the public support by the Catholic and Presbyterian churches should have been a tip-off. The real force behind it was the insurance industry trying an early tactic to avoid liability for clergy abuse.

I objected to the bill as follows in my FindLaw.com column of Aug. 16, 2001:

Although the Catholic Church now supports an obligation to report child abuse in Massachusetts, in Colorado it
[and the Presbyterian Church] has supported a "no fiduciary duty" bill that would make churches immune from
damage awards in cases where they knew of the clergy
malpractice and child abuse.

\*\*\*

Here we have the specter of two mainline, powerful
churches intent on protecting their coffers when one of their
own abuses a member. They are asking the legislature to
remove an extraordinarily strong deterrent to hiding abuse:
legal and financial liability.[12]

The Colorado fiduciary duty bill was an early, bold, and
experimental move by the insurance industry to reduce
its financial exposure in cases involving errant clergy and
knowing religious organizations before the public was aware
of the problem. And it almost worked. Even the legislators did not fully understand the impact of the bill, and
the public certainly had no idea how prevalent clergy abuse
was. That was still the era when most of us believed that
a church would never hide the identity of a child predator – churches protected children; that was their job. (In
2008, it is awfully hard to remember those halcyon days,
isn't it?)

Had the bill passed, there can be little doubt that the
insurance companies would have pushed similar legislation
in every state. Fate (and a very close vote), however, stopped
that particular train from moving down the track, leaving

churches liable in most states in some way for negligent supervision and other torts like fraud when they placed their employee predators near children.

## Insurance Interests Have Been Raised as a Shield against SOL Reform in Ohio, Pennsylvania, and Delaware

Three states – Ohio, Pennsylvania, and Delaware – have had very different experiences with proposed window legislation and the insurance industry. The window legislation was a victim of legislative skullduggery in Ohio, was delayed in Pennsylvania, and succeeded in Delaware. Insurance lobbyists active in all three states.

### Ohio

Ohio, which I will discuss in more detail in the next chapter, was a brutal testing ground for survivors, who were finding healing through public action only to have the Republicans and bishops pull their SOL bill out from under them. While "[t]he Ohio Senate unanimously passed Senate Bill 17 [window legislation] in March [2005] . . . it . . . stalled in the House [in part] over concerns about . . . whether it would have wider negative impacts on the state's insurance industry."[13] While advocates for survivors spent the vast majority of their time trying to persuade legislators and parry the bishops, the insurance lobbyists quietly flexed their muscles and, ultimately, assisted in the death of the bill on Mar. 28, 2006.[14]

## Pennsylvania

In Pennsylvania, window legislation was first introduced following the release of the stunning Grand Jury Report of the
Philadelphia District Attorney's Office on the prevalence of
clergy abuse and cover-up in the Philadelphia Archdiocese.[15]
The Report generated momentum for a number of reforms.
After the reform bill percolated for a while in Harrisburg,
the press noted that the window's "future [was] uncertain
because of opposition by the Pennsylvania Catholic Conference and the concerns of insurance companies that represent
dioceses."[16]

The only public sponsor of the window legislation at that
time was Rep. Douglas Reichley (R-Berks/Lehigh), who char-
acterized it as a "last resort."[17] He looked at the bill as lever-
age to force the church to "strongly consider" establishing a
survivors' compensation fund. In other words, he sought to
keep the issue wholly private and only was willing to back
legislative reform in order to persuade the church to set up a
private fund. That way, the insurance industry's criticisms
would be mooted, and the hierarchy could control payouts to
survivors. (From the perspective of survivors, compensation
funds have been woefully underfunded and inadequate to
address their need for their day in court.)[18]

The primary problem with such arguments, though, is
that a Catholic Church fund is only going to provide for
survivors of sexual abuse in connection with the church.
Most survivors of childhood sexual abuse – who desperately
need SOL reform – have absolutely nothing to do with the

hierarchy of the Roman Catholic Church or any church, for that matter. Their perpetrators are family and family acquaintances. So even if a diocese has put together the best victims assistance program anywhere, it hardly makes a dent in the problem. Say someone fixes the Catholic Church system to perfection; even if that happens, we will continue to neglect millions of survivors and fail to learn the identities of millions of perpetrators. SOL reform is pending in the Pennsylvania legislature as of spring 2008, and legislators need to understand the truth: At this point in our understanding, reform is only marginally about the church; it is really about justice for all survivors, who need the insurance industry to increase disincentives to all abuse.

### Delaware

Delaware provides an excellent example of the Catholic hierarchy publicly "carrying water" for the insurance lobbyists. When SOL reform (abolition of the civil SOL plus a window), titled the "Child Victims Act," was pending in Delaware, Tony Flynn, a lead lawyer for the Wilmington Diocese, argued against it, charging that evidence would be too old or nonexistent in many cases[*] and that the insur-

---

[*] This is a silly argument coming from churches (and other employers). The Roman Catholic Church, for example, has kept "secret archives" that pristinely preserve decades-old employment records proving that their predator priests were (1) abusing children; (2) the hierarchy knew as much; and (3) the hierarchy's answer was to move the priest around to other dioceses. The window

ance industry relies on SOLs. According to Flynn, "Insurance programs and risk management are all predicated on what the statutes of limitation are. If you buy insurance and the rules change, you're stuck."[19] Additionally, "Matthew C. Doyle, commercial marketing executive for the Zutz Group insurance firm, said only a handful of insurers will write supplemental coverage for sexual abuse and molestation liability in Delaware. He predicted that such coverage would be prohibitively expensive for some groups, and some organizations catering to youth and children would be forced to shut down for lack of insurance."[20] The insurance companies did not bother to supplement their public positions with facts – in virtually every settlement between the dioceses and clergy abuse survivors, insurance companies have paid half of the damages awarded, and they have remained in business despite these payments.

During the hearings in the full House, the sponsor of the bill, Rep. Deborah Hudson (R-Fairthorne) commented that SOL reform also appeared to be a moneymaking proposition for the insurance industry, a point to which I will return at the end of this chapter.[21]

In the end, despite "an [insurance] industry representative warn[ing] of the potential for higher-cost or nonexistent insurance coverage,"[22] the Delaware reform bill eventually

---

legislation in California has proven these facts repeatedly. But for the window legislation, and the survivors' resulting lawsuits, most of the truth would still be secret.

passed, due to the concerted efforts of two visionary legislators – Sen. Karen Peterson (D-Stanton) and Rep. Hudson –
and by a coalition of organizations called Child Victims
Voice. This organization kept the spotlight on the fact that
the reform bill was legislation for children and child sex
abuse survivors. The lobbyists' attempts to hog the spotlight failed when the needs of the survivors for a day in
court and society's need to identify perpetrators surfaced.
Sen. Peterson put it like this: "This law belongs to the children of Delaware, who as children had no voice. Now, they
have a voice."[23]

## The Insurance Industry's Knee-Jerk Reaction to the Clergy Abuse Crisis and SOL Legislative Reform May Be Wrongheaded as a Business Model

The insurance industry's lobbyists have been heavy lifters
in the construction of the high wall that this society has
built around predators, which protects and empowers those
predators against public judgment. If the survivors are shut
out of court, the insurance companies do not have to pay
on the premiums that employers paid to cover for abusive employees – because no one knows who did what to
whom! So, at least for the time being, the status quo –
short SOLs and hidden predator identities – serve insurance industry interests. It will take a lot of work on the
part of visionary legislators and pioneering survivors (with
their allies and families) to overcome the sad alliance

between the insurance industry and the churches on these issues.

Let me end this chapter the way I started it: Follow the money. Is it really in the insurance industry's interest to try to block SOL reform for child sex abuse? While there may be some increased liability in the short term, the industry may be standing at the threshold of increasing its profits significantly. If the SOLs are eliminated, every private and public entity will need coverage for its employees who work with children. That sounds like more policies and more premiums to me. At the same time, the industry will ensure that there are fewer claims, as it does in every other category, including health care and automobile safety. When it is constructing its contracts, the insurance industry normally brings in the experts, determines how to reduce the bad acts that make it liable, and thus improves the odds for safety, health, and welfare. For example, the insurance industry has lobbied heavily for automobile seat belt and motorcycle helmet legislation – there is no question that both moves have increased safety and reduced social cost, including cost to the insurance business. So this may well be a growth opportunity for the insurance industry and an opportunity for this country to make children safer.

SOL reform helps the insurance industry reduce its risk in the following ways:

(1) More perpetrators are publicly identified, making it harder for those perpetrators to create more victims

in the future, reducing the number of claims and the amount of risk.

(2) The industry can condition coverage explicitly on companies and individuals taking positive actions that reduce the incidence of abuse, for example, they can say they will refuse coverage if a company fails to report known perpetrators to authorities or places a known predator in another position close to children.

(3) The industry can, in turn, reduce the cost of medical insurance and the high cost to society arising out of child sex abuse by helping to reduce the incidence of abuse.

In short, the insurance industry could be a crucial and effective player in the larger social network needed to reduce and maybe even eliminate childhood sexual abuse.

SOL reform is an opportunity for the insurance industry to reduce health costs, to increase profits, and to make children safer. Thoughtful insurance executives need to rethink their knee-jerk opposition to SOL reform.

# 6

## Barrier #2

## The Hierarchy of the Roman Catholic Church

In 2002, a dark cloud arrived on our shared horizon with the first publication, by the *Boston Globe*, of the stories of hierarchical cover-up of clergy abuse within the Roman Catholic Church's Boston Archdiocese. The *Globe*, which won a Pulitzer Prize for its coverage,[1] set into motion a mind-boggling series of revelations: The next reports involved the Diocese of Manchester, New Hampshire, and eventually the dioceses of a long list of cities (see Appendix A to Chapter 6).

For the Catholic hierarchy, though, the issue has remained solely an issue of "us against them." Their focus has led them to fight reform that would benefit all survivors of child sex abuse, most of whom have had nothing to do with the Church.

## The Experiences of the Roman Catholic Church Have Educated the Public on the Pervasiveness of Child Sex Abuse and the Failures of the Legal System

The Roman Catholic Church is the largest religious denomination in the United States, with 64 million members, or 22 percent of the U.S. population.[2] Other than the federal government,[3] it is difficult to imagine an institution in the United States that can match its presence, reach, or influence. By comparison, the largest U.S. corporation, measured by number of employees, is Wal-Mart Stores with 1.8 million.[4] Even when compared at the international level, the church is huge. The Holy See is an independent sovereign, with 1.1 billion believers, constituting about one-sixth of the world's population.[5] There are 18,584 Catholic parishes and 41,794 priests in the United States alone.[6] If there is an institution-wide policy within an organization of this size – like hiding the identities of child-molesting clergy – it likely affects every state, if not every county, which means no American is terribly far from feeling its effects, whether Catholic or not.

Several factors have contributed to the Roman Catholic Church's role in teaching us what we need to know about arbitrary and unfair statutes of limitations (SOLs) governing child sex abuse. First, it is an easily visible body. Second, its sheer weight makes a quick shift in the institution's policies and practices impossible; once the public's attention is caught, it cannot change rapidly enough to hide otherwise unthinkable secrets. In fact, when the Boston Archdiocese and its hierarchy found themselves in the glare of public scrutiny in 2002, the hierarchy momentarily froze and then never did succeed in pushing all of their secrets back into the dark. The scandal could not be buried once it broke.

The lessons learned from the Catholic hierarchy extend to all institutions dealing with children. Therefore, studying the hierarchy's actions creates a "teaching moment" for the country, and even the world. The same pattern of abuse, institutional knowledge, and concealment are seen in a surprising array of private and public organizations. Three examples make my point.

First, in the secular public sphere, the Texas Youth Commission was unmasked in February and March 2007 by reports that its supervisors were sexually abusing children within the system, which consisted of thirteen schools educating 3,000 juvenile delinquents or inmates under the age of twenty-one. The abusers' superiors covered up the abuse.[7] The supervisors were not reported to authorities and were permitted to resign quietly, and even after employees complained, no action was taken for at least a year.[8] The same deficiencies in the law and social attitudes that have failed these survivors of childhood sexual abuse fail most survivors.

Second, the same archetype of institutional knowledge of abuse and cover-up can be found among Jehovah's Witnesses. Bill Bowen, a former Jehovah's Witness member turned activist for the survivors, has established an extraordinary Web site, www.silentlambs.org, which has followed the subterfuge in his former church. Thousands of survivors have contacted him, and more news from here and abroad appears on a regular basis.

Third, the Boy Scouts have followed the same precedent – knowledge of abuse within the organization followed by cover-up. Numerous cases have been filed against Boy Scout leaders[9] and most recently it was estimated that over 5,000 Scout leaders have been removed to date.[10]

There is also emerging and important data about abuse coverup in the public schools.

These are just discrete examples – the model of knowledge and cover-up of sex abuse is not peculiar to any of these institutions. It is part of the fabric of our society, reinforced by overly short SOLs. But it is the Roman Catholic hierarchy that is putting the most resources into fighting SOL reform at this time.

### What we have learned from the Roman Catholic Church's hierarchy is applicable to all private institutions, including other religious organizations

There is a curious and pervasive social phenomenon of hiding abusers' identities, which is nondenominational and hardly limited to religious organizations. When the Southern Baptist Convention was called to account in February 2007 for reports that there was child abuse by pastors who were then moved to other churches, it did not embrace responsibility for a culture that permitted children to be abused. For example, Debbie Vasquez told how she was raped by Rev. Dale "Dickie" Amyx at Bolivar Baptist Church in Sanger, Texas, when she was fifteen years old. Those in power at Bolivar Baptist forced her to atone for her sins as an unwed mother in front of the congregation, but never told the congregation that their minister was to blame for the pregnancy.[11]

It may seem like a counterintuitive response, but the standard answer by an organization confronted with a pattern of child abuse within its boundaries is to claim that it had no choice – it could not prevent the abuse. The Baptist Convention's answer was that it could not do anything, because of the decentralized structure of the church. Unlike the Catholic Church, Southern Baptist churches are independent entities that operate largely free from control of a central body.

In comparison, Catholic bishops have argued that they could do nothing about predatory priests (other than move them from parish to parish), because of their belief in forgiveness and reconciliation and the hierarchical character of the Church: No one was supposed to interfere with a bishop's oversight of a priest's "formation."[12] Of course, this is all poppycock – institutions (whether hierarchical or decentralized) can establish sound programs to detect and deter child abuse. They must, however, have the will to do so.

Speaking as an observer of these phenomena, the standard objection to SOL reform is fear of false claims against adults. This is a straightforward example of adults rushing to prefer adults' interests over children's interests. The data, at least in California, show that the concern is overblown. There were about a handful of false claims attempted in California, out of the over 1,000 claims made during the window's effect. That is one half of one percent. When compared with the fact that 300 new predators were identified to the public, the scale weighs more heavily on the children's side and away from this particular objection.

Certainly, not all churches have shrugged off their moral responsibility: The Presbyterian Church's system is considered the gold standard.[13] Even so, the Presbyterian Church has had its abusers.[14]

It is a supreme irony that we have been educated about the prevalence of child abuse and the failures of the legal system by the Catholic Church's hierarchy. We know we need SOL reform because of them, but they are working feverishly to prevent new SOL reform for child sex abuse survivors.

### The reality: SOL reform is all about children, not the Church

SOL reform will protect all children and deter perpetrators as well as any institutions aiding them. The 70 to 80 percent of survivors who were abused by family or family friends need it just as much as the hierarchy's victims. But the Catholic hierarchy has lobbied as though theirs was the only entity affected.

"The problem in Harrisburg [Pennsylvania] is that powerful lobbies want to make it look like this is a plan or a program against one institution," [District Attorney Lynn]

Abraham told a conference at Temple University's Beasley School of Law. "But this is about children."[15]

## The big lie: reforming the law for child sex abuse survivors will destroy the Church

"When a certain amount of time passes, it becomes impossible to defend yourself," said Dennis Poust [spokesperson for the New York State Catholic Conference]. "This is simply trial lawyers trying to enrich themselves by taking advantage of a tragic thing that happened."

Some of the cases in California were as much as 70 years old, he added.

And while "many lawyers perceive the church as having deep pockets," suspending the statute of limitations could cripple the good works of dioceses across the state, Poust said. "It could have disastrous implications for the church's charitable ministries and its educational ministries," he said.[16]

The hierarchy of the Roman Catholic Church – the cardinals, bishops, and their dioceses – has expended unconscionable amounts of money and time trying to block reform of SOLs. They were still off balance following the *Boston Globe*'s 2002 public revelations of the Boston Archdiocese clergy abuse cover-up when the California window was enacted and put into effect in 2003. Once they realized what the California window meant – their many secrets spilled publicly after their victims entered the courthouse – they fought like mad to (1) get the window declared unconstitutional, (2) establish a constitutional right to keep their personnel files privileged, and (3) prevent window legislation in other states. We will never know just how much they have spent on legal counsel to attack the window, but it easily runs into the tens of millions of dollars.

### California set the stage for survivors to be able to get into the courthouse, and the dioceses made one desperate move after another to keep them out

As just over 1,000 victims filed through the 2003 California window to access the justice system, survivors in other states started to mobilize, and the hierarchy assumed a nation-wide defensive posture. The California Diocese cases were consolidated into three regional districts: Northern California, Southern California, and Los Angeles and Orange counties.[17]

The California window law applied to "any person or entity" that might have caused the abuse in some way.[18] There was no language whatsoever that limited the window's impact to the Catholic Church alone.

Yet, in each region, the diocese's lawyers heatedly argued that the window was unconstitutional because it "targeted" the Catholic Church. Even though the language of the law was not aimed at any one single institution or entity, and roughly 150 individuals filed suits against entities not affiliated with the Catholic Church, the hierarchy took the narcissistic view that it was aimed at them, and, therefore, the

Church's constitutional right to freely exercise its religion was being violated. (If the law were "targeting" a single religious institution, it would be unconstitutional because the government is required to be neutral.) However, the state and federal courts were not persuaded and upheld the window against one constitutional attack after another.[19] The courts consistently found that the legislation was aimed at a wide variety of institutions and that the effect on the Catholic hierarchy had less to do with targeting than their own bad acts.

The many filings against the California dioceses do not prove targeting but rather spotlight the scope of abuse within the institution. California legislators had learned from the Church's public struggle with clergy abuse that the law needed to change, but its solution extended well beyond the Church's victims. The dioceses were not targeted by this neutral legislation. The tragedy of the California window is that it was so short (only twelve months), which meant that many meritorious claims were not filed because the survivor did not know about or understand the window.

Four-and-a-half years after the California window closed, I published an editorial in the *Los Angeles Times* praising the California legislature for passing the window after the Los Angeles Archdiocese settled with more than 560 survivors for roughly $1.3 million apiece.[20] In response, I heard from a number of survivors of non-Catholic organizations, including various cults and the Buddhist Church, who suddenly understood what they had missed long after the window closed. Thus, the window's opening in California did not reach a significant number of survivors. One year might be long enough in other states, especially if the legislation is well-publicized before passage, but in California, many survivors were caught unaware and unable to file a claim before the window shut again.

Nearly 850 Californians used the 2003 window to file civil suits against the Catholic hierarchy and dioceses for hiding the identities of child predators within the organization and, therefore, placing children in dire harm's way. In addition, approximately 150 survivors filed suits against defendants who were completely unrelated to the Catholic Church. A *Los Angeles Times* article named the Boy Scouts of America, the Explorers,[*] the Salvation Army, and the Seventh-day Adventist Church as some of these other defendants.[21]

Many other survivors were not able to take advantage of the open window before it shut after only one year. For example, the tragic survivors of the Children of God (later called The Family) missed the opening. *Rolling Stone* magazine covered the suffering of some of the members of the Children of God, a despicable sex cult that started in Berkeley, California, settled in Brazil and Argentina,[22] and then fanned out around the world. The *Rolling Stone* article cited

---

[*] A Los Angeles Police Department program, and also a part of Boy Scouts of America, designed to provide youths with an opportunity to explore careers in law enforcement.

the example of the cult's founder's granddaughter, Mene, who, "by the age of eleven, in 1983 . . . was drinking wine and watching adult videos at a [cult] facility in Greece. Later at his compound in the Philippines, a drunken [cult leader] repeatedly fondled her." When that cult leader's wife became jealous and worried that Mene would become his next wife, she engaged "in a [cult] practice called Teen Training, [where] Mene suffered vicious physical abuse. . . . In Macau, Mene was locked in a room for six months. She was tied to a bed and beaten, thrown against walls and even forced to undergo multiple exorcisms."[23] By the early 1990s, Mene was institutionalized.[24] Other survivors were subjected to sex with adults when they were toddlers and on-demand sex from adults during their adolescence.[25]

The true (and sad) story about the California window is how inadequate it was for most childhood sex abuse survivors: Many were not ready to come forth publicly by the end of the year, including so many of the victims of incest or of family "friends." The Catholic Church hierarchy's victims were on alert because of a historical accident – extensive media coverage about the cover-up of abuse in the Catholic Church – while most of the other child sex abuse survivors were oblivious through no fault of their own. This was the first major window at a time when there was only limited awareness about the barriers childhood sexual abuse survivors face to disclosure. The United States should be grateful to California for leading the way, but this was only the early dawn of the civil rights movement for children.

Luckily, for many of the survivors of the Roman Catholic dioceses, though certainly not all survivors, there was enough public focus on the Church's history that they were attuned to such legislation. In addition, because of the way in which windows operate, once a few Catholic survivors came forward and publicly identified their priest perpetrators, others soon followed. A window's ripple effect is extraordinary – approximately 300 new perpetrators were publicly identified in California.

### The California courtroom wars over window legislation

The Church hierarchy's lawyers fought every aspect of the California window cases: They spent years plotting to keep their "secret archives" secret, fabricated new "privileges" to avoid court-ordered discovery of their files,[*] and argued that the window was unconstitutional. In the end, the lawyers lost their legal battle, but in the process, they and their clients, the dioceses, inflicted on the survivors yet more delay and another level of Dante's *Inferno*.

---

[*] My personal favorite was the so-called formation privilege, which was concocted in Southern California and was intended to keep the courts from ordering discovery of any materials related to a bishop's "formation" of a priest's vocation. The courts quickly divined that the "formation privilege" was intended to cover all personnel files of abusive priests – and rejected it. *See* Roman Catholic Archbishop of Los Angeles v. Superior Court, 131 Cal. App. 4th 417, 427 (Cal. Ct. App. 2005). *See also* Michael Rezendes, *Bid to Shield Priest Data Faulted*, BOSTON GLOBE, March 14, 2003, *available at* http://www.poynter. org/column.asp?id=46&switch=true&DGPCrSrt=&DGPCrPg=373.

The window was in effect only one year after the *Boston Globe* fallout. There was a keen national and statewide focus on the sins of the Catholic hierarchy, with the *Los Angeles Times* aggressively covering the cases, the emerging facts, and the new survivors coming forward. Although the Church's argument about unconstitutional targeting was not thrown out by the courts as frivolous, it should have been. The Church hierarchy wrapped itself in the First Amendment's freedom of religion clauses, arguing that California could not pass a law affecting it so directly. I collaborated in crafting much of the constitutional strategy for the survivors in California and was thrilled when the following (and plainly correct) decision was handed down by a federal court in the *Melanie H.* case, which I briefed and argued:

> The Court concludes that [California's window legislation] does not burden the choice, supervision, or retention of priests. A review of the statute itself does not reveal any reference to or attempt to regulate a religious practice or belief. Third party liability for sexual assault does not implicate or effect any religious belief, opinion, or practice. The failure to supervise or negligent hiring of a person that commits sexual assault does not implicate or effect any religious belief, opinion, or practice. SB 1779 [the window] regulates only conduct that the State is free to regulate. The Court concludes that SB 1779 is a general law, not aimed at the promotion or restriction of religious beliefs.[26]

California state courts also upheld the window, which led to settlements in Northern California (averaging approximately $1.1 million/survivor),[27] Orange County ($1.1 million/survivor),[28] Los Angeles ($1.3 million/survivor),[29] and San Diego ($1.4 million/survivor).[30]

## The California Model Is Opposed in Other States

As the hierarchy watched the wheels of justice turn in California, the bishops mobilized their forces. The lobbying arm of the hierarchy, the U.S. Conference of Catholic Bishops (which is composed of the bishops across the country), went to work behind the scenes and in the press to prevent any other windows from opening. For childhood sexual abuse survivors, the bloodiest battlegrounds were Ohio and Colorado in 2006.

### The Ohio sleight-of-hand

The hierarchy of the Catholic Church is no different from any other determined legislative player – if it cannot win on its own merits, dirty tricks will do. Survivors of clergy abuse spent two solid years of their lives talking to Ohio legislators, attending hearings, and holding rallies to make the point that child sex abuse survivors deserve SOL reform and window legislation. It was one of the most impressive grassroots movements I have ever witnessed. The Senate passed the bill unanimously. But the bishops held the upper hand, and late on the night the window bill was supposed to finally pass in the Ohio House, the bishops succeeded in making the bill disappear.

The Survivors Network of those Abused by Priests (SNAP) were early proponents of SOL reform beyond California and fought hard in Ohio to get a window passed. The proposed law extended the SOL for all current and future childhood sexual abuse claims, and, like California's law, opened a one-year window during which the SOL did not apply. The proposed law also mandated that clergy, like others who come into contact with children in their jobs, must report childhood sexual abuse.[31]

In the Ohio Senate, the stars aligned for SNAP perfectly. An Ohio resident and firefighter, Tony Comes, recently had been the subject of an Academy Award–nominated HBO documentary, *Twist of Faith* (2004).[32] I was there the day the Senate passed the window legislation unanimously – March 16, 2005.[33] Mr. Comes spoke, and senators spoke movingly, as did several current Catholic priests (including Father Mark Schmeider of Cincinnati, Father Steven Stanberry of Toledo, and Father Gary Hayes of Paducah, Kentucky),[34] who themselves had been abused as children by clergy.[35] Survivors filled every available seat, wearing lanyards with pictures of themselves as children. Survivors clapped and cried; it was deceptively easy to believe that the bill would sail through the House as well. That did not happen.

In the House, the opposition began in earnest. I suppose no one will ever know the actual motives of the chairman of the House Judiciary Committee, John Willamowski

(R-Lima).[36] He had one meeting after another with the survivors, telling them he was on their side, but then he also held meetings with those in opposition, which included the Catholic Conference of Ohio and Bishop Frederick Campbell of Columbus, who promoted the dioceses' contemporary actions, "including the removal of 25 priests from ministry in Cleveland alone; mandatory criminal background checks on new employees seeking to work with children; child-abuse awareness training for diocesan workers; and creation of independent councils to investigate abuse."[37] Campbell's testimony also revealed that financial concerns, such as the loss of insurance coverage, were playing a role in the Catholic Church's attack on the legislation.[38]

The Ohio Catholic Conference also pushed an argument that the window was unconstitutional under the Ohio Constitution. Then Willamowski gathered everyone – pro and con – around a large conference table in the House for a series of meetings. I attended a few of the meetings to explain why the bill was constitutional. Willamowski's theory appeared to be that there was a middle ground only he could find if he just forced the two sides to meet often enough.

SNAP pushed for a public hearing and got one on Nov. 10, 2005. One panel addressed the hierarchy's argument that the window legislation was unconstitutional. I testified in favor of the bill while Professor Christopher Fairman, of Ohio State University School of Law and Timothy Luckhaupt, the Ohio Catholic Conference lobbyist, argued against the one-year window for three main reasons, none of which have proven to be true, though they were enough to defeat the window in Ohio:

> *It's unfair.* Going back 35 years means applying what we know today about pedophiles to a time when more people believed they could be treated and returned to the ministry. *It's unconstitutional.* And even if some people disagree, lawmakers should wait to see what the Ohio Supreme Court does with two pending cases involving people who sued the Catholic Church after the statute of limitations ran out. *It's unnecessary.* The Catholic Church has taken a number of steps to prevent future sex abuse, including sex-abuse awareness training, and many dioceses have published the names of priests found to have committed sex abuse.[39]

Days after the hearing on whether the window was constitutional, on Nov. 22, 2005, there was a second hearing in front of the House Judiciary Committee where approximately 115 survivors and supporters were in attendance. For almost twelve hours, with only a forty-five-minute lunch break, the committee heard testimony from forty-one individuals, out of the sixty-seven who were prepared to testify.[40] One survivor stated that he was sexually molested by his Cincinnati Catholic high school principal the day after his father died of cancer.[41] The courageous and outspoken Bishop Thomas J. Gumbleton revealed that he himself had been molested and stated his unequivocal support for a one-year window: "First of all, I am here because there is still the strong likelihood that some perpetrators have not yet been brought to account. That is why I support the one-year civil window. I do believe that the abusers need to be exposed. I also believe that this can only be assured if the possibility exists to bring these matters into a civil court of law. By doing this we will increase, as far as humanly possible, the protection from becoming victims of sexual abuse that all children have a right to."[42]

Survivors were hopeful. However, the night the window bill was supposed to pass on the floor of the Ohio House, the Republicans went into caucus and reappeared with a substitute bill. The window had disappeared and was replaced with the bishops' choice, which guaranteed survivors would not be compensated. Local newspapers noted that the substitute bill had removed the "looking back" provision of a one-year window. In its place now is a worthless and probably unconstitutional civil registry of sex offenders.[43] The substitute bill would allow an offender's name to be placed on the registry after a judicial determination that a victim had been sexually abused, even if the offender has never been criminally charged. The offender would then have to report an address and employer. The survivor would only be able to collect legal fees.[44] Barbara Blaine, a survivor of clergy abuse in Ohio, and president of SNAP, stated that "this registry is a shallow, empty promise that will provide no measure of protection for children or justice for survivors."[45] She was right, of course.

So much for fair play when the issue is childhood sexual abuse in Ohio.

### The orchestration of opposition in Colorado

The hierarchy undoubtedly was quite pleased with itself after its "victory" in Ohio, but the method of execution was unlikely to be capable of repetition in other states. The Ohio window legislation was conquered through political cunning and cunning alone. In the next battleground, in Colorado in 2006, the hierarchy started to craft a more portable and comprehensive battle strategy to vanquish legislation liberalizing the SOLs for childhood sexual abuse. Their unlikely leader was Denver Archbishop Charles Chaput.

Chaput was originally from Kansas, chose his vocation at age thirteen, joined the Order of Friars Minor Capuchin, St. Augustine Province, in 1965, and was educated at St. Fidelis College Seminary in Herman, Pennsylvania; Catholic University; Capuchin College; and the University of San Francisco. He began as a parish priest, moved up in the Capuchin organization, graduated to Bishop of Rapid City, South Dakota, and eventually graduated to his position in Denver.[46] He is described as "an affable and vigorous [man] and a genuine 'people-person'" with a commitment to youth that has "led him to challenge young people wherever he went to have joy and hope in a radical commitment to Jesus Christ."[47] That commitment did not extend to survivors of childhood sexual abuse when advocates sought to open the courthouse doors for them. Quite the contrary, in fact.

By 2005, there was an obvious need for legislative reform in Colorado, where the SOL on negligence claims was only two years. Father Harold Robert White was the subject of approximately fifteen lawsuits filed against the Denver Archdiocese – one initiated by his own godson, Delbert C. Nielsen[48] – for molestation that took place between the early 1960s and early 1980s. According to one of the survivors, White told him that the abuse was "the will of God." White's was the classic clergy abuse story: the hierarchy learned about the abusing cleric and responded by moving him from parish to parish. White served in eleven parishes across Colorado between 1960 and 1993, and the lawsuits allege that the archdiocese hid prior allegations "to protect White, conceal its own wrongdoing and prevent lawsuits."[49] A number of these cases have been resolved in mediation with the archdiocese, while the remaining three unresolved cases were parceled out among Denver district judges. (In March 2007, Denver District Judge John McMullen denied the Church's motions to dismiss the suits, clearing the path for all three to move forward.[50]) Stories like White's spurred Colorado legislators, especially Senate President (and devout Catholic) Joan Fitz-Gerald (D-Coal Creek Canyon), to take action and back SOL reform.

Archbishop Chaput can hardly be given sole credit for routing the Colorado bill, but he does get points for hiring one of the pricier public relations firms (Phase Line Strategies, a high-powered lobbying firm with ties to Gov. Bill Owens)[51] and then implementing their public relations plan. The strategy was an innovative twist on the California hierarchy's argument that window legislation is unconstitutional because it "targets" the Catholic Church. Through flyers placed in the pews each Sunday for parishioners, Chaput argued that window legislation was bad because it did not apply to public institutions. Phase Line Strategies and Chaput knew full well that the bill would apply beyond the Church to all private institutions but claimed there was a fatal defect, because it did not extend to public institutions. (If you had to read that sentence twice, you now know what I was thinking the first time I heard the argument! What?!) It was not that there was any sincere concern about protecting all of Colorado's children; rather, they were taking a calculated risk – if they argued that the bill should be extended to reach public institutions, the hierarchy could achieve three key objectives: (1) the bill would appear to be unfairly narrow making it less likely to pass even when it did not target the Church; (2) parishioners would be misled into thinking that the "real motives" behind the bill must be anti-Catholic, which would mobilize a grassroots campaign against the window bill; and (3) those opposed to a more extensive bill, such as teachers' unions, would be mobilized to defeat such reform. They wanted to kill the bill, but managed to sound as though their genuine concern was children and fairness. They gained allies in parish and legislative hallways all while sounding like they actually were trying to protect children. One has to give them credit: This was a brilliant, if utterly devious, move.

On Jan. 31, 2006, Chaput, Colorado Springs Bishop Michael Sheridan, and Pueblo Bishop Arthur Tafoya issued the following statement:

> The evidence is . . . irrefutable that sexual abuse and misconduct against minors in public schools is a serious problem – in fact, more serious than anywhere outside the home, including churches. . . . Since most Catholic children in Colorado attend public schools, this should seriously concern the whole Catholic community. . . . Too many public authorities have had too little accountability on the issues of sexual misconduct and abuse for too long. . . . As a society, if Coloradans are really serious about ending the sexual abuse of minors, that needs to change. . . . Catholics need to demand from Colorado lawmakers an end to our state's legal inequities in dealing with childhood sexual abuse.[52]

The leader of the Colorado opposition, Chaput, laid out their insidious strategy as follows:

> Of course, certain crimes are so terrible, like murder, that no statute of limitation is warranted. Some people argue that the sexual abuse of minors is such a crime. Catholics don't necessarily oppose that approach. Many Catholics are parents. They very rightly sympathize with victims and

want to protect their own children. But the Catholic community does insist that all such laws, reporting timeframes and penalties apply equally to everyone and every institution, with no hidden escape clauses.... Unfortunately, most state laws don't treat public and private entities equally when it comes to claims arising from the sexual abuse of children. In almost every state, public officials use a combination of governmental immunity, very brief reporting timeframes and very low financial damage caps to make it difficult for anyone to sue public institutions – including public schools.[53]

It was not that Chaput was lobbying in favor of including public schools in the reform legislation; he was just interested in pushing aside the legislation altogether. As David Clohessy, national director of SNAP, put it, Chaput is a "Johnny-come-lately" to the issue of sex abuse in schools. Clohessy termed the argument "a ruse, a diversion designed to derail the effort."[54]

The Colorado Catholic Conference also personally attacked the Catholic legislators who backed the legislation. For example, Gwyn Green, a first-term Democrat in the Colorado House, was "appalled by the viciousness of the personal attacks the church made" on her for her advocacy of the window legislation. "They read letters denouncing me from the pulpit . . . and what they said was totally untrue."[55] The Catholic Conference also made sure that she learned that they planned to throw their resources into defeating her in the next election.[56] Fitz-Gerald (president of the Senate) also was treated in an ugly fashion. She described how difficult it was "sitting at Mass on Sunday and having the work you're doing to protect children mischaracterized.... This is about children... who were shamed by the acts done to them.... They went through life wondering what they did to deserve either rape or sodomy or both."[57]

Chaput played the "fairness" card over and over again, but his winning argument to his parishioners was composed of outright lies about the effect of reform on the financial health of the Catholic Church. Every large settlement in the church's clergy abuse arena has been paid as follows: Roughly half from insurance, and the remainder from the sale of property that is not dedicated to religious use, for example, office buildings and parking lots.[58] Charitable public works are not affected by these settlements: Catholic Charities' funds come overwhelmingly from the government (depending on the state, 70–90 percent).[59] As Cardinal O'Malley in Boston has explained, closures of parishes have not arisen from payments to the survivors; rather, the need to do so has arisen from less giving from parishioners and the usual demographic changes that require reorganization of parochial schools.[60] The facts, however, have not stopped those like Chaput from fighting legal reform by triangulating the survivors against the parishioners:

"Unless Catholics wake up right now and push back on behalf of their church, their parishes and the religious future of their children, the pillaging [of church resources] will continue," Chaput said in an e-mail response to questions posed by *Our Sunday Visitor*, a national Catholic weekly. Bishops, said Chaput, "have a duty to protect the heritage and patrimony of the Catholic community that laypeople have worked so hard though the decades to build up."[61]

There is not a more vile strategy out there. Unfortunately, it worked.

Once the Colorado House rejected the window legislation on May 4, 2006, the momentum to alter the SOL for child sex abuse died. A survivor expressed his frustration:

"I want to say to the legislators that the pedophiles out there are cheering in your favor. They're saying, 'I'm home free,'" said Brandon Trask, 49, who sued, claiming former priest Harold White repeatedly molested him in Minturn and in the Glenwood Springs baths during the 1970s. "(Archbishop Charles) Chaput has spent more money defending his pedophiles. . . . Money talks, and the little ones walk."

The Colorado Catholic Conference, through its spokesperson Tim Dore, stayed on message: The survivors don't matter, but "fairness" to the Church does:

We have been clear and open about our concerns with this unfair legislation and will continue to do so, so long as it unfairly targets the Catholic Church.[62]

The truth is that they were not "clear and open" about their ultimate goal: killing all legislation that would alter the SOL for child sex abuse. They never introduced a comprehensive bill covering both private and public entities or a companion bill covering the public entities.

Their argument also rested on the false assumption that a legislature must fix every aspect of a problem in a single bill. As I explained in Chapter 4, the law is usually divided into two separate spheres – private and public. Reform with respect to child abuse is needed in both, but that does not mean it has to happen simultaneously. It is not unfair to include churches with private institutions, which is what the proposed Colorado window legislation would have done.

### Delaware: the Colorado strategy fails and the survivors win

Delaware was the first state to pass window legislation after California's model. On July 10, 2007, Gov. Ruth Ann Minner signed the Child Victims Act into law and restarted the momentum toward a national movement to free child sex abuse victims from arbitrary and unfair SOLs.[63] The key to success was putting the public focus where it belonged: on all survivors of childhood sexual abuse.

Anthony Flynn was the flunky for the Catholic Diocese of Wilmington, who stated in May 2006 that "the diocese would 'vigorously oppose' any effort to revive claims already barred by the statute of limitations."[64] Taking their cue from Denver's Chaput, those advocating for the Church pulled out the fairness card, but this time it did not work. An extremist organization called the American Society for the Defense of Tradition, Family, and Property took out a full-page advertisement in the Wilmington newspaper the *Delaware News Journal.* According to the group, the legislation was really a "veiled persecution of the Church." The organization further tried to triangulate parishioners against survivors, saying that Church property would be "confiscated" to pay settlements. As Father Tom Doyle pointed out, these statements were filled with lies and demonstrated a vile and "hostile attitude toward victims of clergy abuse."[65]

By May, as the bill gained credibility and momentum, the Catholic Diocese of Wilmington, represented by Flynn at an eight-hour hearing held by the House Judiciary Committee, trotted out the usual lies about "potential ministry cutbacks." This time, the lies did not prevail, and the committee voted unanimously in favor of sending the bill to the full House.[66]

The result in Delaware is directly attributable to the joining together of a diverse coalition of organizations, which made nearly impossible the diocese's effort to persuade anyone that the legislation was solely aimed at it. Child Victims Voice, the coalition formed to advocate for the legislation, includes almost 100 nonprofits and various religious denominations.[67] (A complete list of coalition members appears in Appendix B to Chapter 6.)

The coalition drowned out the diocese, which eventually pulled back from its opposition to eliminating the civil SOL. (It never backed off its opposition to the window, though.) When the diocese announced it was no longer opposed to the reform of the civil SOL, it also pulled a move straight out of Chaput's pocket: It tried the "fairness" card, saying that state institutions and private institutions should receive identical treatment (with the hope that bundling the two spheres would result in killing the bill completely).[68] Rep. Greg Lavelle (R-Sharpley) served as the diocese's errand boy and tried to introduce an amendment that would remove sovereign immunity from state entities, but the amendment was defeated at the full House hearing, because it needed further study.[69]

Lavelle took the "fairness" argument to a new low when he showed up at the hearing with a double frame, containing pictures of his two children. One, apparently, attends public school and the other attends private school. He asked witnesses which child in the frame should get the better treatment, essentially telling them to choose between his two children. He had very little success, and I thought the move was so sleazy and offensive that he would have abandoned it by the time I testified toward the end of the full House hearing. He asked me about the fairness of treating public and private institutions separately, and I responded that reform was needed in both arenas, but the law had always treated public and private entities independently. Therefore, Delaware should take up the issue separately. When he pulled out the photos during my testimony, the mother in me took control. I told him the question was "ridiculous" and "stupid." No one would want either of the adorable children in those pictures to suffer. But he is an elected representative, and he has an obligation to carefully consider these issues in their separate arenas – private and public.

When Lavelle realized the vote in the House was going to be unanimous in favor of the bill, he changed his original vote from "no vote" to "pass."

Not only did the coalition make a difference in Delaware, but Sen. Karen Peterson (D-Stanton) and Rep. Deborah Hudson (R-Fairthorne) were remarkable and dogged leaders in their respective houses. Voice of the Faithful was very active and held a memorable celebration after the bill-signing. Said John Sullivan, one of the founders of the Coastal Delmarva chapter of Voice of the Faithful, "This battle's over, but there are many others.... This is a wonderful day for the children of Delaware and hopefully for the entire nation. This sets the example for the rest of the states to do the right thing for children.... Now, it's time to celebrate."[70] Sullivan and other supporters celebrated Mass with Father Richard Reissmann, pastor of St. John the Baptist–Holy Angels, and shared a covered dish supper.[71] One survivor and his family, too, were tireless in forming the coalition and contacting allies like me. That survivor, Matt Conaty, deserves a lot of credit for fighting this particular battle. In his own words, "You transform from a victim to a survivor when you are able to use your voice."[72]

## The Catholic hierarchy has proved itself irrelevant to the question of statute of limitations reform for all child sex abuse survivors

When I testified in the District of Columbia in favor of SOL reform for child sex abuse survivors, I had an epiphany – the Catholic Church is actually irrelevant. In the big picture, it is responsible for only a small fraction of the total number of child sex abuse survivors, and, as a society, we owe every survivor a day in court. In effect, each diocese was lobbying to kill reform that would aid incest survivors, those abused by family, friends, and online predators. Kowtowing to it would be an abdication of responsibility to the vast majority of survivors, who are unrelated in any way to the Catholic Church.

The archdiocese had its two representatives there, and they argued that the District of Columbia Archdiocese has done such a great job in taking care of survivors that no window was needed. That is unlikely, but if even they have handled in-house cases perfectly, that is no argument to stop the child abuse legal reform movement. The Catholic Church does not deal with or treat those survivors it had no hand in creating, so to use its "good record" to demonstrate that there is no need for reform legislation is just illogical, not to mention immoral.

# 7

## The Other Barriers

### Teachers, Defense Attorneys, and an Uninformed Public

The only thing necessary for the triumph of evil is for good men to do nothing.

Edmund Burke

A staggering fact is that children are most at risk of sex abuse when we think they are safest: at home, at school, and at church. Worse, many of the folks we would assume are lobbying our state legislators to protect children, like parents, teachers, lawyers, and civil rights groups, are actually working against victims of child sex abuse in the legislative context. In this chapter, I will unmask the enemies to legislative reform beyond the insurance industry and the Roman Catholic Church: teachers (and their unions), defense attorneys (including civil liberties groups), and a woefully uninformed public.

## DEEPLY ROOTED SOCIAL PRACTICES HAVE CREATED THE CONDITIONS THAT VICTIMIZE SO MANY CHILDREN

The statistics in Chapter 1 are worth repeating: studies say about at least 25 percent of girls and 20 percent of boys are sexually abused, and 90 percent of abuse is never reported to authorities. It takes the commitment of an entire culture to repress, hide, and permit the suffering of so many people.

As has been documented again and again, the Roman Catholic Church has engaged in an orchestrated cover-up of child abuse; the same can be said for a number of other religious organizations, such as the Church of Jesus Christ of Latter-day Saints (the Mormons), the Jehovah's Witnesses, the Southern Baptists, and many others. Why so many religious organizations? Because they are fertile ground for predators intent on obtaining unquestioned access to children. The religious sphere is just the beginning, though; school systems and many others also have fostered the conditions that make childhood sexual abuse victims second-class citizens whose needs are pushed to the very bottom of the public agenda. (At least until now.)

## THE TEACHERS

When everyone learned about the Catholic Church hierarchy's cover-up of horrific child abuse, first in Boston and then throughout the United States, there was palpable shock. How could the people who are supposed to be the most trustworthy souls anywhere – Roman Catholic priests – actually abuse children? Worse, how could the majestic-looking bishops protect the predators at the expense of the children?

This tragedy was so unfathomable that there are Catholics even today who have not been able to accept the ugly reality. Believing that the whole crisis stems from greed or anti-Catholic bias is much easier than confronting the reality that there are tens of thousands of suffering individuals whose abuse is a result of their own church's actions to cover up the identity of predators. I will talk about the dangers to children of such an uninformed public at the end of this chapter, but first I want to zero in on the fact that the Catholic hierarchy does not stand alone in its instinct to hide the truth about child sex abuse. Adults in many circumstances have weighed their personal interests more heavily than the needs of children, and the law has been structured to aid them as it oppresses the victims.

## A School District and Union Unify Behind Hiding the Identities of Abusing Teachers

It would have been nice if we had walked away from the Catholic Church hierarchy's scandal with a confident conclusion that all we would need to do is to assist those victims and prevent the hierarchy from repeating its crimes and torts. Unfortunately, the Catholic hierarchy's orchestration of abuse is just one example among others.

It is hard to gauge where the problem is worse – in church or at school – but suffice it to say that children are at risk, period. Some have said that "[t]he problem in education dwarfs the Catholic Church problem."[1] Others disagree. For example, a spokesperson for the Colorado Education Association said that "[i]n a school situation, when a teacher or a employee is accused, or even some little hint comes along there may be a problem, schools and districts react so quickly, our lawyers say they're assuming guilt and are almost ripping them out of the classroom... From everything I've read, the (Catholic) church has pretty much tried to sweep these issues under the carpet, and I don't think that's the case at all in schools."[2] The difference in treatment is due in part to individual state and local laws, some of which give religious organizations special treatment. That helps them avoid liability, as I document in *God vs. the Gavel*. There are a variety of approaches to regulating state and local institutions. What we know for sure is that children can be at serious risk in both public and private environments.

The instinct to cover up seems to be strong in many circumstances, and teachers' unions accentuate that instinct. The *Seattle Times* requested information on public school teachers and was surprised when the Bellevue School District, which is east of Seattle, did not treat its request as routine. The state supreme court, after all, had ruled in 1990 that teachers have no right to privacy with respect to records involving sexual misconduct with students and, therefore, the records should be made available to the public.[3] Despite the earlier ruling, "[t]he Bellevue teachers union organized a district-wide personnel-file review so teachers could go through their files and remove materials."[4] The *Times* did succeed in getting some of the files released, but only after it initiated litigation.[5]

In other words, even our children's teachers are perfectly capable of making it more difficult to identify child predators. As I discussed in the last chapter, Denver Archbishop Chaput may have had the goal of killing all legislative reform for children in Colorado when he introduced the issue of public school teachers into the debate, but he was correct in the sense that his organization is hardly the only one placing children at severe risk.[6]

The similarities between the Church hierarchy's and the schools' *modus operandi* with respect to child abuse is striking. As one newspaper put it, "[s]exual misdeeds by teachers remain a dirty little secret in schools across the nation."[7] There are definite parallels to the churches' situation: "What makes [sexual abuse of students by teachers] so traumatic is the violation of the sacred trust. The sacred trust placed in teachers is no different from that placed in parents, priests or ministers."[8] There is another parallel in that, like the churches, the schools fail to identify perpetrators to the public and "deal with" abusing employees by moving them from one school to another. As one mother of a victim put it, "We call that passing the trash...One bad teacher can molest many, many children."[9]

Just like the religion context, most child predators' identities in the schools have never been identified to the public. Hofstra University Professor Charol Shakeshaft says that only 10 percent of such abuse ever gets reported.[10] Few school predators' names are published on Megan's Law lists. For example, in West Virginia, from 2000 to 2005, 41 teachers lost their licenses for sexual assault or abuse, but "only four are on the state police's sex offender Web site."[11]

Nor are the schools doing a good job of communicating their knowledge of child predators to the public. Terri Miller, president of Stop Educator Sexual Abuse, Misconduct and Exploitation, a New York-based nonprofit advocacy group, says that schools and local governments often do not report abuse, even in states where reporting is mandated.[12] Moreover, background check requirements can be gutted by teacher union lobbying. In West Virginia, for example, new teachers must undergo background checks, including an FBI fingerprint check, but the teachers' union succeeded in creating an exemption for such checks on existing teachers (unless they are moving outside the county where they have been teaching).[13] Ironically, there is a national database of teacher license revocations, but the content is kept confidential.[14]

Professor Shakeshaft has generated some truly disturbing facts. In a 1994 study, she determined that out of 225 cases of teacher sex abuse in New York, zero were reported to the authorities and only 1 percent of the teachers were deprived of their licenses. The few who were reprimanded received very light punishments, with a full 25 percent receiving no consequence or an informal reprimand. As in the clergy context, those who left carried with them positive letters of recommendation to their next jobs. Others reported that in the state of Washington, confidentiality agreements with abusers were still used by school districts, and resignations were secured by promising positive letters of recommendation. Plus, there is plenty of evidence that school districts, like churches, willingly keep such records secret and maintain known abusers on the job.[15]

I will leave it to the sociologists and psychiatrists to explain *why* rational, well-educated adults, who have devoted their lives to serving children, react to evidence of abuse by protecting the accused abuser's reputation and sublimating the needs of children to be protected from predators. It makes no more sense than the religious organizations' cover-up of abuse. We do know there is a tendency not to report an abuse to the authorities if we know the person well.[16] Beyond that, there is much to be studied.

## Teachers' Unions Have Opposed Legislative Reform for Victims of Child Sex Abuse

Teachers' unions have conflicting instincts and agendas in this area. On the one hand, they exist to protect their members' jobs, but on the other hand, they also advocate for the protection of children in many contexts. To date, when these two interests collide, as they do in the context of statute of limitation (SOL) reform, they have chosen their members' interests at the expense of children.

As an example, the Illinois Federation of Teachers Department of Political Activities sometimes works for chidren's interests and sometimes for teachers'. It has pushed for legislation that will "protect and enhance the professional integrity and bargaining rights of all members."[17] For example, it has sought to protect members in circumstances where the Department of Children and Family Services is investigating child abuse. At the same time, the organization works to "[s]trengthen child labor laws and oppose economic exploitation and abuse of children"; lobbies for adequate public services for "child welfare"; and lobbies "to ensure that schools are safe havens for students and school employees."[18] This latter item, in particular, would seem to indicate that the federation is a natural ally for children and victims of child sex abuse.

The Maryland State Teachers Association was an ally to the Catholic Conference in Maryland when it fought to the death a bill that would have strengthened child abuse reporting requirements and reformed the SOL in 2003.[19] Between the Catholic Conference, the teachers, and the defense attorneys, whom I will discuss in the next section of this chapter, child sex abuse victims have had no chance at legal reform in Maryland.

The obstacles to reform created by the teachers and their representative organizations are similar in many ways to those imposed by the Catholic Church, producing similar results. There has not been adequate reporting of child sexual abuse by teachers or punishment of the perpetrators. At the same time, there have been pro-active efforts on their part to block access to records and lobby against legislative reforms. As with many obstacles to child sexual abuse reform, the problem is that the focus is on the adult teachers as employees and not on the children they serve.

Truth be told, the role of school teachers and their unions with respect to SOL reform is still an evolving story. The major player trying to block such reform to date is the Roman Catholic hierarchy, which means other groups, like teachers, only have played a supporting role. Teachers still have plenty of time to choose the side of the angels.

## THE DEFENSE ATTORNEYS

Defense attorneys, obviously, represent those who have committed the crime or the tort, for example, the child predator and his or her enablers. It should not come as a surprise that they have opposed legislation that protects children from abuse. They have opposed mandatory child abuse reporting;[20] increased sentences and supervised release periods for convicted sex offenders;[21] and child abuse SOL reform, too.[22]

### Defense Attorney Opposition to Legislation Reforming the Statute of Limitations for Child Sex Abuse

The defense attorneys' objections to criminal SOL reform were recently summarized by the State of Connecticut's Division of Public Defender Services as follows:

> [W]ithout a limitation period, evidence may be unable to be located, destroyed or may deteriorate. In addition, memories of witnesses fade and sometimes no longer exist. It may be difficult or impossible to locate witnesses who may have moved or have passed on. Without any finite period of time within which a prosecution can be brought, it may be impossible for an innocent person to fairly defend himself, 30, 40, 50 or more years beyond the date of the offense.[23]

The curious part of this critique is that the burden is on the government in the first instance to prove a criminal case beyond a reasonable doubt. If there is no evidence, or if the evidence is weak, the extension of the SOL has no effect, and the defendant wins. The underbelly of the argument, though, is this: the vast majority of child sex abuse crimes never get reported, because the SOL is too short for the victims to come forward. For those victims in cases with good evidence, even if that evidence is old, the prospective abolition of the criminal SOL puts more perpetrators in jail and many more names on the Megan's Law lists. We are all safer then. Defense attorneys have yet to explain how they can oppose laws that are so effective in protecting our children.

Defense attorneys also have opposed civil SOL reform. When reform was pending in Colorado, one respected defense attorney turned to attacking the victims, saying, "Priests who violated children should be prosecuted . . . But I think we're way beyond that now. We're now heavily into the greed factor."[24] This is a sad statement by an attorney, because it intentionally mixes apples and oranges in the law to mislead the public in favor of child predators. In fact, most predator priests could not be prosecuted, because the criminal SOL had run out long before the victim came forward, and the United States Supreme Court ruled that legislatures may not open a criminal window, as I discussed in Chapter 4. Civil suits are their only option.

The Maryland window bill was opposed by defense attorneys as well and, in particular, the Maryland Defense Council, which is composed of 650 civil defense attorneys.[25] The American Civil Liberties Union has an abysmal record when it comes to children. When given a choice, the ACLU and its state affiliates seem automatically to choose adults' interests over those of children; attempts to persuade the ACLU to take up children's rights as a separate issue have faced stiff opposition within the organization. This unfortunate reality was highlighted again when the Civil Liberties Union of the National Capitol Area took a position against window legislation in the District of Columbia. In typical fashion, the civil liberties group weighed the interests of the adults against the interests of the children and preferred the adults. The organization wrote: "Crimes against children are despicable. At the same time, the rights of the accused are precious . . . there is no reason further to undercut the ability of persons to defend themselves."[26] No account was taken of either the prevalence of abuse or the difficulties child sex abuse survivors have coming forward.

## AN UNINFORMED PUBLIC

The final hurdle to protecting children is an uninformed public. It has taken an entire country to create a favorable environment for the wide-scale child sex abuse present in the United States, and real change likely will be impossible without better public education and legislative leadership. Sadly, the public has been repeatedly misled by those affected by such reform: the churches, the teachers, and the defense attorneys. Father Tom Doyle stated the need for public education as follows: "The experience with the Catholic Church has proven this denomination and other denominations as well as other private and public institutions will only change when forced to do so by a power greater than themselves – and that power has been the media, public opinion and especially the U.S. legal system."[27]

A significant obstacle for those advocates, like me, intent on changing the SOLs to benefit child sex abuse victims is that those opposed often take advantage of an uninformed public to make their cases. In Colorado, reform was stopped cold by Denver Archbishop Chaput's "appeal" to his parishioners, whom he inundated with the standard arguments against such legislation: supposedly, the bill targeted the Church, would bankrupt the Church, and was unfair to defendants. The Colorado public had no way of knowing that the arguments he raised were filled with misleading innuendo, crafted with public relations, rather than children, in mind.

The one group of child sex abuse victims that has succeeded in some measure to educate the public about their plight consists of the victims of clergy abuse. The Survivors Network of those Abused by Priests (SNAP) and Link-Up have developed good relationships with the media and have done all victims of such abuse a service by educating the public on the legal and moral challenges victims face. Link-Up has seen a "seismic shift in public opinion."[28] This segment of the abused population, though, is relatively small. Studies and education on the experiences of incest and family acquaintance victims – the largest group of those abused – is seriously needed.

The single most important legal reform for all victims lies in eliminating the SOLs for all victims of sexual abuse. The challenge lies in explaining to the public what this rather dull area of the law actually does, and why this seemingly bland timing mechanism can generate so much injustice. SOLs are procedural timing rules that determine when one can go to court; when they expire, they have the effect of locking the courthouse doors and throwing out the keys. These are not difficult concepts, but they are not part of most Americans' typical education.

One law professor stated, "We [as a society] have mixed feelings about statutes of limitations . . . We have them for good reasons, but in an individual case, it often feels like an unjust result to some people when a prosecution is thrown out."[29] In my experience, few have any feelings on SOLs because they know nothing about them! As I discussed in Chapter 3, there are very good reasons for SOLs in cases involving property or money. We need stability and pre-dictability to be able to sustain our active and complex eco-nomic universe. But there is no good reason to barricade the courts against victims of sex abuse. Perpetrators and their enablers do not deserve predictability or stability in their lives.

The best means of returning stability to the victims is to give them their day in court when they are ready. Visionary legislators will have to sift through the knee-jerk opposi-tion of the insurance industry, the churches, teachers, and defense attorneys to get to the correct public policy balance. Both state and federal governments need to invest resources in educating the public about the reality of child abuse in the United States, so that those lobbying against children will not have the upper hand.

# Conclusion

## The Coming Civil Rights Movement for Children

Children, especially child sex abuse victims, are at such an enormous disadvantage in the United States. They have been locked out of the justice system again and again, while we have permitted – consciously or unconsciously – predators to live free from public scrutiny. The simple change of eliminating the statutes of limitations (SOLs) turns that set of relationships upside down, placing the child sex abuse victims in the position of power.

It is sad that children's interests have been such a low priority on both the right and the left. The right has championed "parents' rights," which would keep the government out of what they consider family business. While individuals can disagree on what amounts to "spanking" or inappropriate discipline, the political right undermines its own "family values" rhetoric if it extends those principles to the child sex abuse sphere.

It is an unfortunate fact that many Republicans to date have resisted SOL reform for child sex abuse victims, in part because Republicans tend to be more beholden to religious interests than others. A shining exception is Rep. Deborah Hudson in Delaware, whose leadership led to unanimous support for SOL reform in the Delaware House.

On the left, the American Civil Liberties Union (ACLU) rarely if ever takes the side of a child (unless it is the right of the child to speak in a public school) and has increasingly taken up the cause of religious organizations.[1] In addition, its focus on old-fashioned civil liberties tends to make it sympathetic to the perpetrator defendants' interest in shorter SOLs rather than the child victims' need for time to come forward. Time will tell whether the ACLU joins the coming civil rights movement for children or is left behind. In the meantime, the Civil Liberties Union of the National Capital Area actively opposed SOL reform in the District of Columbia, as I discussed in Chapter 7.

To reiterate, the national tragedy of widespread child sex abuse deserves more sustained examination in every quarter. It is morally reprehensible to take a position that prefers predators to children. There is certainly no constitutional right that would force us to favor predators over children.

Not so long ago, children were the property of their parents. The revelations of child sex abuse and the work done in the past twenty years to increase child safety indicate that a civil rights movement for children is afoot. Children deserve far more protection. Their need to be protected from adult sexual attack and exploitation should be at the top of every political party's agenda – at least as high up the list of priorities as children's need for health care coverage.

The failure to account for the rights of children is a national, pervasive problem. As one victim recently wrote:

> While being shocked by a local case of an area student allegedly sexually abused by a school custodian is understandable, no one should be shocked that [it] is happening to children in general. The sexual abuse of children is a societal problem not limited to any one part of our nation, any class of people, or any single institution. It happens in our schools, churches, homes, daycares and our workplaces.
>
> By some estimates there are over 39 million survivors of childhood sexual abuse in America today – and I am one of them.[2]

If I have made my case as persuasively as I hoped, my reader should know that the United States has structured itself to date in a way that subverts the interests of children. We have ignored and suppressed the needs of the millions of childhood sexual abuse victims. It is not just that the topic has been taboo (though that is surely part of it) but that the legal system systematically has preferred the interests of adults over the needs of children. We have been living in a dual-class culture, where adults have rights and legitimate demands but children are part of a lesser class. The topic of their general social status is well beyond the scope of this book, but this factor is surely an element in the wayward construction of a legal system that perversely benefits predators and continually victimizes childhood sex abuse survivors.

There is a dawning understanding that we simply cannot afford to keep the secrets that protect adults and forsake children. A secret ocean of suffering exists, which increases health care costs, reduces the productivity of millions of individuals (to the detriment of us all), and generates untold suffering for families and friends. The system simply cannot continue, because it costs too much.[3]

It is a fact that the authorities and the law must be a central part of any movement to create greater safety for children. The Catholic Church's problems have shown, repeatedly, how private concealment of the identities of child predators increases the danger to all children exponentially. Each time a predator priest has been given the hierarchy's blessing to move onto the next assignment and to "sin no more," while the public was told nothing about the priest's record, new children were fondled, raped, or sodomized. It is still happening. Father McCormack of the Chicago Archdiocese pled guilty in 2007 to sexual assault of a child in 2006. He was available to abuse that child because Chicago Cardinal Francis George did not tell authorities about McCormack when he first learned about his propensities. Secrecy about child predators within a private system is a guarantee of more abuse, more suffering, and a greater cost to society. Only when one of the abused boys told his mother, and they went to the authorities, did the balance shift in favor of children. There must be a public side to any child abuse prevention program for it to succeed.

## Legislative Reforms to Date for Childhood Sexual Abuse Victims Are Inadequate to Reduce the Incidence of Childhood Sexual Abuse – SOL Reform Is Needed to Make Them More Effective

If one examines the "solutions" to date for child sex abuse – harsher punishments, pedophile-free zones, and Megan's Laws – it is readily apparent that we are suffering from tunnel vision. The purpose of these laws is to limit the damage done by already known perpetrators and that is laudable. But, until the SOLs are eliminated, we will not know the identities of most predators.

The time has come to look to the survivors themselves and give them what they need most: their own day in court. When these victims finally have a true opportunity for justice – because the arbitrary SOLs have been removed – all of society will benefit.

California has led the way, with Delaware following. They deserve tremendous credit for taking the side of childhood sexual abuse survivors against formidable odds.

Every other state needs to follow their lead. Then, and only then, will the survivors receive long overdue justice and the public learn who are the predators in our midst.

It is an either/or choice: we can protect the predators or the children.

# Appendix to Chapter 4

## Statutory Language

### ABOLITION OF CRIMINAL STATUTE OF LIMITATIONS

(1) ALABAMA: "(a) There is no limitation of time within which a prosecution must be commenced for: (4) Any sex offense involving a victim under sixteen years of age, regardless of whether it involves force or serious physical injury or death." ALA. CODE §15-3-5 (2007).

(2) COLORADO: COLO. REV. STAT. §16-5-401(2) (2007).

(3) DELAWARE: DEL. CODE ANN. tit. 11, §205(e) (2007).

(4) MARYLAND: absence of any limitation by statute.

(5) SOUTH CAROLINA: absence of any limitation by statute.

(6) WYOMING: absence of any limitation by statute.

### NO CRIMINAL STATUTE OF LIMITATIONS FOR ASPECTS OF CHILD SEX ABUSE

(1) No Limitation for any felony child sexual abuse: KENTUCKY KY. REV. STAT. ANN. §500.050 (2007); NORTH CAROLINA N.C.

GEN. STAT. §15-1 (2007); VIRGINIA VA. CODE ANN. §19.2-8 (2007); WEST VIRGINIA W. VA. CODE §61-11-9 (2007).

(2) No Limitation for most forms of child sexual abuse: ALASKA ALASKA STAT. §12.10.010 (2007); IDAHO IDAHO CODE ANN. §19-402 (2007); MAINE ME. REV. STAT. ANN. tit. 17, §A-8 (2007); MISSISSIPPI MISS. CODE ANN. §99-1-5 (2007); RHODE ISLAND R.I. GEN. LAWS §12-12-17 (2007).

## ABOLITION OF CIVIL STATUTE OF LIMITATIONS

(1) DELAWARE: (a) A cause of action based upon the sexual abuse of a minor by an adult may be filed in the Superior Court of this State at any time following the commission of the act or acts that constituted the sexual abuse. A civil cause of action for sexual abuse of a minor shall be based upon sexual acts that would constitute a criminal offense under the Delaware Code." Child Victims Act, S.B. 29 w/HA 3, 144th Gen. Assem. (Del. 2007) (enacted, to be codified at DEL. CODE ANN. Tit. 10, §8145).

(2) MAINE: (1) No limitation. Actions based upon sexual acts toward minors may be commenced at any time. ME. REV. STAT. ANN. tit. 14 §752-C (2007).

(3) ALASKA: (a) A person may bring an action at any time for conduct that would have, at the time the conduct occurred, violated provisions of any of the following offenses: (1) felony sexual abuse of a minor; (2) felony sexual assault; or (3) unlawful exploitation of a minor. ALASKA STAT. §09.10.065 (2006).

## DELAYED DISCOVERY LEGISLATION

(1) MINNESOTA: (a) An action for damages based on personal injury caused by sexual abuse must be commenced within six

years of the time the plaintiff knew or had reason to know that the injury was caused by the sexual abuse. MINN. STAT. ANN. §541.073 (2007).

(2) CALIFORNIA: (a) In an action for recovery of damages suffered as a result of childhood sexual abuse, the time for commencement of the action shall be within eight years of the date the plaintiff attains the age of majority or within three years of the date the plaintiff discovers or reasonably should have discovered that psychological injury or illness occurring after the age of majority was caused by the sexual abuse, whichever period expires later..." CAL. CIV. PROC. CODE §340.1 (2007).

## WINDOW LEGISLATION: TWO-YEAR WINDOW

(1) DELAWARE: (b) For a period of two years following the effective date of this bill, victims of child sexual abuse that occurred in this State who have been barred from filing suit against their abusers by virtue of the expiration of the former civil statute of limitations, shall be permitted to file those claims in the Superior Court of this State. *Child Victims Act*, S.B. 29 w/HA 3, 144th Gen. Assem. (Del. 2007) (enacted, to be codified at DEL. CODE ANN. Tit. 10, §8145).

(2) MINNESOTA: Notwithstanding any other provision of law, a plaintiff whose claim is otherwise time-barred has until August 1, 1990, to commence a cause of action for damages based on personal injury caused by sexual abuse if the plaintiff proves by a preponderance of the evidence that the plaintiff consulted an attorney to investigate a cause of action for damages based on personal injury caused by sexual abuse within two years of the time the plaintiff knew or had reason to know that the injury was caused by the sexual abuse. Minn. Stat. 541.073, sec. 7 (1989); Amended: 1992 – Laws 1992, c. 571,

art. 12, §2, amended Laws 1991, c. 232, §5 to provide: "Notwith-standing any other provision of law, a plaintiff whose claim would otherwise be time-barred under Minnesota Statutes 1990 has until August 1, 1992, to commence a cause of action for damages based on personal injury caused by sexual abuse if the action is based on an intentional tort committed against the plaintiff."

(3) DISTRICT OF COLUMBIA'S Proposed Language: (11) For recovery of damages from any person or entity related to child-hood sexual abuse – within six years of the time that the victim fully comprehends the causal connection between the sexual abuse which occurred as a minor and the injury resulting from such abuse. The time of comprehension shall be determined by a jury upon medical or psychological testimony. Sec. 3. Applica-bility Section 1 of this bill applies to any criminal cases pend-ing on the effective date of this act and any criminal cases that are brought after the effective date of this act for which the applicable time limit for prosecution has not yet run. Sec-tion 2 of this bill applies to any civil claim that is pending on or commenced on or after the effective date of this act regard-less of whether a previous statute of limitations expired before enactment of this law.

## WINDOW LEGISLATION: ONE-YEAR WINDOW

(1) CALIFORNIA: (c) ... [A]ny claim for damages described in paragraph (2) or (3) of subdivision (a) that is permitted to be filed pursuant to paragraph (2) of subdivision (b) that would otherwise be barred as of January 1, 2003, solely because the applicable statute of limitations has or had expired, is revived, and, in that case, a cause of action may be commenced within one year of January 1, 2003. Nothing in this subdivision

shall be construed to alter the applicable statute of limitations period of an action that is not time barred as of January 1, 2003. CAL. CIV. PROC. CODE §340.1 (2007).

## NATIONAL SEX OFFENDER REGISTRATION

(1) FEDERAL: Sec. 113(a) "A sex offender shall register, and keep the registration current, in each jurisdiction where the offender resides, where the offender is an employee, and where the offender is a student. For initial registration purposes only, a sex offender shall also register in the jurisdiction in which convicted if such jurisdiction is different from the jurisdiction of residence." Adam Walsh Child Protection and Safety Act of July 27, 2006, Pub. L. No. 109–248, 2006 U.S.C.C.A.N. (120 Stat. 587).

# Appendixes to Chapter 6

## APPENDIX A*

Alexandria, Allentown, Amarillo, Archdiocese of Anchorage, Archdiocese of Atlanta, Altoona-Johnstown, Arlington, Austin, Baker, Archdiocese of Baltimore, Baton Rouge, Belleville, Birmingham, Bismarck, Boise, Bridgeport, Brooklyn, Brownsville, Buffalo, Burlington, Camden, Charleston (South Carolina), Charlotte, Cheyenne, Archdiocese of Chicago, Archdiocese of Cincinnati, Cleveland, Columbus, Corpus Christi, Covington, Crookston, Dallas, Davenport, Archdiocese of Denver, Des Moines, Archdiocese of Detroit, Archdiocese of Dubuque, Duluth, El Paso, Erie, Evansville, Fairbanks, Fall River, Falls-Billings, Fargo, Fort Wayne–South Bend, Fort Worth, Fresno, Gallup, Galveston-Houston, Gary, Gaylord, Grand Rapids, Green Bay, Greensburg, Harrisburg, Archdiocese of Hartford, Helena, Honolulu, Houma-Thibodaux, Archdiocese of Indianapolis, Jackson, Jefferson City, Joliet, Juneau, Kalamazoo, Archdiocese of Kansas City (Kansas), Kansas City–St. Joseph (Missouri), La Crosse, Lafayette (Indiana),

* http://bishop-accountability.org/priestdb/PriestDBbydiocese. html#KS.

Lafayette (Louisiana), Lansing, Las Cruces, Las Vegas, Lexington, Lincoln, Little Rock, Archdiocese of Los Angeles, Archdiocese of Louisville, Madison, Marquette, Memphis, Metuchen, Archdiocese of Miami, Archdiocese of Milwaukee, Archdiocese of Mobile, Monterey (California), Nashville, Archdiocese of New Orleans, New Ulm, Archdiocese of New York City, Archdiocese of Newark, Norwich, Oakland, Ogdensburg, Archdiocese of Oklahoma City, Archdiocese of Omaha, Orange County (California), Orlando, Owensboro, Palm Beach, Paterson, Pensacola-Tallahassee, Peoria, Phoenix, Archdiocese of Philadelphia, Pittsburgh, Portland (Maine), Archdiocese of Portland (Oregon), Providence, Pueblo, Raleigh, Rapid City, Reno, Richmond, Rochester, Rockford (Illinois), Rockville Centre, Sacramento, Saginaw, Salina, Salt Lake City, San Angelo, Archdiocese of San Antonio, San Bernardino, San Diego, Archdiocese of San Francisco, San Jose, Archdiocese of Santa Fe, Santa Rosa, Savannah, Scranton, Archdiocese of Seattle, Sioux City, Sioux Falls, Springfield (Illinois), Springfield (Massachusetts), Springfield–Cape Girardeau (Missouri), Spokane, St. Augustine, St. Cloud, Archdiocese of St. Louis, Archdiocese of St. Paul–Minneapolis, St. Petersburg, Steubenville, Stockton, Superior, Syracuse, Toledo, Trenton, Tucson, Tulsa, Venice (Florida), Archdiocese of Washington D.C., Wheeling-Charleston (West Virginia), Wichita, Wilmington, Winona, Worcester, Yakima, Youngstown.

## APPENDIX B: CHILD VICTIMS VOICE COALITION MEMBERS*

American Academy of Pediatrics Delaware Chapter

American Association of University Women (Coastal-Georgetown branch)

---

\* Child Victims Voice, http://www.childvictimsvoice.com/supports.html.

Associated Builders and Contractors, Delaware

Bethel Baptist Church (Wilmington, Delaware)

Big Brothers Big Sisters of Delaware

Carl Schnee, Esq., former U.S. Attorney

Charles F. Gallagher III, Deputy District Attorney, Philadelphia
District Attorney's Office

Child, Inc.

Children & Families First

Christopher A. Coons, New Castle County Executive

Common Cause of Delaware

Concord Presbyterian Church, Wilmington, Delaware

Contact Lifeline, Inc.

Daybreak Counseling Services

Dee's Gift

Delaware Association for Children of Alcoholics

Delaware Coalition Against Domestic Violence

Delaware Ecumenical Council on Children and Families

Delaware Governor Dale E. Wolf

Delaware Governor Russell W. Peterson

Delaware Governor Sherman W. Tribbitt

Delaware Mental Health Counselors Association

Delaware Nurses Association

Delaware State AFL-CIO

Delaware State Dental Society

Delaware State Fraternal Order of Police

Doris Schnee, LCSW

Dr. Carol A. Tavani, neuropsychiatrist

Dr. Michael F. Whitworth

Dr. Richard Gartner, author, psychologist, past president of
National Organization on Male Sexual Victimization

FixtheLaw.org

Foundation To Abolish Sex Abuse, Inc.

Fritz Ackerman, pastor, Concord Presbyterian Church

Girls Incorporated of Delaware

J. Roy Cannon, CADC, LPCMH, ACS – Counseling Resource
Associates, Inc.

Jack A. Markell, Delaware State Treasurer

James and Susan Kallstrom, former Assistant Director of the FBI

James L. Ford III, Mayor of Lewes

James M. Walsh, PhD, LPCMH

Jesus House Prayer & Renewal Center

Jewish Family Services

Joseph and Lori Ozdowy, plant manager, DaimlerChrysler
Newark Assembly Plant, Newark, Delaware

Joseph W. Mitchell, president, Mitchell's Inc. (Mitchell's Trains,
Toys & Hobbies)

Judge Louis Freeh, former FBI Director

Lawrence M. Sullivan, Esq.

Lieutenant Governor John Carney

Limen House for Men

Limen House for Women

Marilyn Van Derbur, former Miss America, incest survivor,
advocate for all victims of child sexual abuse

Martha H. Ireland, PhD, RN, CS, CEDS – ADE, Inc.

Matthew P. Denn, Delaware's Insurance Commissioner

Matthias B. Donelan, MD, associate professor of surgery,
Harvard Medical School

Members of Ocean View Presbyterian Church

Michael P. Walsh, Sheriff Of New Castle County

National Eating Disorders Association

PA-C.A.R.E.S. (Pennsylvania Child Abuse Reporting and
Enforcement Strategy)

Prevent Child Abuse Delaware

Prison Ministries of Delaware, Inc.

Professor Marci A. Hamilton, Constitutional law expert

Progressive Democrats for Delaware

Rabbi Sanford Dresin, President of the Rabbinical Association of Delaware

Reginald C. Irby, Executive Director of Limen House for Men

Rescue & Recovery International, Inc.

Rev. Jonathan Baker, senior pastor, Aldersgate United Methodist Church, Wilmington, Delaware

Reverend Thomas P. Doyle, OP, author, canon lawyer

Richard and Bernard Kenny, owners of The Kenny Family ShopRites of Delaware

Richard T. Christopher, President of Patterson-Schwartz Real Estate

Sara E. Whitworth, RN

Sexual Abuse Prevention Network

Sister Jeanne F. Cashman, OSU, executive director of Sojourners' Place

Sister Maureen Paul Turlish SNDdeN, victims' advocate

SNAP (Survivors Network of Those Abused by Priests)

SOAR, Inc. (Survivors of Abuse in Recovery, Inc.)

Sojourners' Place, Wilmington, Delaware

Stop Child Predators.org

Supporting K.I.D.D.S.

Susan O'Connor, RN

Ulster Project Delaware

Voice of the Faithful Affiliate of New Castle County

Voice of the Faithful Coastal Delmarva

Wayne A. Smith, former House Majority Leader

Women's Democratic Club of Delaware

YMCA of Delaware

YWCA Delaware

# Notes

## 1. We Have Failed Our Children

1. E-mail from L. Williams, to Marci A. Hamilton (Oct. 19, 2006, 11:31:41 EST) (on file with author).
2. MARY GAIL FRAWLEY-O'DEA, PERVERSION OF POWER: SEXUAL ABUSE IN THE CATHOLIC CHURCH 6–7 (Vanderbilt University Press 2007) ("almost one third of all girls and up to one fourth of all boys [are abused] before they reach eighteen"). *See also* Jennifer J. Freyd et al., *The Science of Child Sexual Abuse*, SCIENCE, Apr. 22, 2005, at 308 ("Child sexual abuse involving sexual contact between an adult... and a child has been reported by 20 percent of women and 5 to 10 percent of men worldwide. Surveys likely underestimate prevalence because of underreporting and memory failure.... [C]lose to 90 percent of sexual abuse cases are never reported to the authorities," citing World Health Organization, *World Report on Violence and Health* (2002) (*prepared by* Etienne G. Krug et al., eds.)); child sex abuse is a global problem. David Usborne, *UN Report Uncovers Global Child Abuse*, THE INDEPENDENT (LONDON), Oct. 12, 2006, at 28 (150 million girls and 73 million boys under 18 experience forced sexual

intercourse and other forms of sexual violence in 2002); World Health Organization, *Child Sexual Abuse and Violence*, *available at* www.searo.who.int/LinkFiles/Disability,_Injury_Prevention_&_Rehabilitation_child.pdf ("Studies conducted by various NGOs and institutions in 1995 and 1997 respectively in Delhi revealed that more than half the girls surveyed had experienced sexual abuse by family members; 76 percent women across five cities in India admitted sexual abuse as children"); World Health Organization, Division of Family and Reproductive Heath, *Sexual Violence: A Hidden Epidemic*, *available at* http://www.afro.who.int/drh/sexual_violence.html ("7 percent to 36 percent of girls and 3 percent to 29 percent of boys have suffered from child sexual abuse.").

3. Freyd et al., *supra* note 2 ("close to 90 percent of sexual abuse cases are never reported to the authorities").

4. Beth Miller, *Sex Abuse Victims Seek More Time to Sue: Bill Eliminating Civil Statute of Limitations Passes Senate, Goes to House*, News Journal (Wilmington, Del.), Apr. 5, 2007, at 1; Randall Chase, *Del. Senate Passes Bill Extending Time for Sexual Abuse Lawsuits*, AP Alert, Apr. 5, 2007, at DE 00:41:15.

5. Sacha Pfeiffer, *Geoghan Preferred Preying on Poorer Children*, Boston Globe, Jan. 7, 2002, at A1.

6. Pam Belluck, *Bishop Knew Boston Priest Had Praised Man-Boy Sex*, N.Y. Times, Oct. 29, 2002, *available at* http://query.nytimes.com/gst/fullpage.html?sec=health&res = 9807E0DD153FF93AA15753C1A9649C8B63.

7. http://www.boston.com/globe/spotlight/abuse/stories/010702_history.htm (Fr. Geoghan was not transferred outside of the diocese except for treatment); *see also* http://www.boston.com/globe/spotlight/abuse/stories/010602_geoghan.htm.

8. http://www.bishop-accountability.org/assign/Shanley-Paul-Richard.htm (Fr. Shanley was transferred to California. This article provides a timeline of Fr. Shanley's movement).

9. http://www.catholic.org/featured/headline.php?ID = 30.

10. Lynne Abraham, District Attorney, City of Philadelphia, Report of the Grand Jury 23–24 (2005), *available at* http://

www.philadelphiadistrictattorney.com/images/Grand_Jury_
Report.pdf.

11. *Id.*

12. Bruce Lambert, *Case Highlights Sex Abuse at Church, Beyond Priests*, N.Y. TIMES, May 15, 2007, at B4 (mentioning each of these groups and others, including coaches, camp counselors, seminarians, parochial school teachers, day care and health care workers, catechism instructors, and nuns).

13. Roxanne Lieb, Vernon Quinsey, & Lucy Berliner, *Sexual Predators and Social Policy*, 23 CRIME AND JUSTICE 43, 50 (1998). In addition, according to the 1992 Crime Data Brief for the United States Department of Justice, in three states only 4 percent of child rape offenders for female victims under 12 years old were strangers to the victims. Forty-six percent of the offenders were family members of the victim, and 50 percent of the offenders were acquaintances or friends (or other nonfamily relationship) of the victim. For victims ages 12–17, only 12 percent of the offenders were strangers, while 20 percent were family members and 65 percent were friends or acquaintances of the victim. Patrick A. Langan & Caroline Wolf Harlow, *Child Rape Victims, 1992*, CRIME DATA BRIEF, June 1994, NCJ-147001, at 2.

14. Kenneth V. Lanning, "Investigator's Guide to Allegations of 'Ritual' Child Abuse," Behavioral Science Unit, National Center for the Analysis of Violent Crime, Federal Bureau of Investigation (1992).

15. *See* Michael Rezendes et al., *A Revered Guest: A Family Left in Shreds; Church Allowed Abuse by Priest for Years Aware of Geoghan Record, Archdiocese Still Shuttled Him from Parish to Parish*, BOSTON GLOBE, Jan. 6, 2002, at A1.

16. *Id.*

17. Abraham, *supra* note 10.

18. Bruce Murphy, *Murphy's Law: The Catholic Cover-up and the Explosion of Ex-Cons in Milwaukee*, MILWAUKEE MAGAZINE, Feb. 13, 2007.

19. *See id.* (Marie Rohde was pulled off the Widera story by the editor of her paper, the MILWAUKEE JOURNAL SENTINEL).

20. THOMAS P. DOYLE, A.W. RICHARD SIPE & PATRICK WALL, SEX, PRIESTS, AND SECRET CODES: THE CATHOLIC CHURCH'S 2000-YEAR PAPER TRAIL OF SEXUAL ABUSE (Bonus Books 2006).

## 2. What Is Wrong with the System?

1. National Center for the Victims of Crimes, Extensions of the Criminal & Civil Statutes of Limitations in Child Sexual Abuse Cases (2006), http://www.ncvc.org/ncvc/main.aspx?dbName=DocumentViewer&DocumentID=32466. Alabama, Alaska, Kentucky, Maine, Maryland, North Carolina, Rhode Island, South Carolina, Virginia, West Virginia, and Wyoming do not have an SOL for prosecuting sexual offenses. And some of *these* states, like Kentucky, have limited the application of no time limitation to particular offenses or ages of the victims. Some other states have no time limitation for the worst forms of sexual assault regardless of victim age, including Florida, Indiana, Mississippi, New Jersey, New Mexico, and South Dakota.

2. The United States Supreme Court first applied the discovery rule in *Urie v. Thompson*, 337 U.S. 163 (1949), though not for child sexual abuse. The case of *Tyson v. Tyson*, 727 P.2d 226 (Wash. 1986), decided in 1986, was one of the first cases to address the discovery rule issue in childhood sexual abuse cases. While *Tyson* no longer represents the current law in Washington State, parties on both sides of the discovery rule issue still use it as persuasive authority when making their claims. In *DeRose v. Carswell*, 242 Cal. Rptr. 368 (Ct. App. 1987), it was argued and okayed in dicta but held not to apply in the situation. In *Bassile v. Covenant House*, 575 N.Y.S.2d 233 (Sup. Ct. N.Y. County 1991) and *Schmidt v. Bishop*, 779 F. Supp. 329–30 (S.D.N.Y. 1991), New York courts held that there is no "discovery rule in this class of cases." A federal court in Illinois has held that Illinois courts would apply the discovery rule to cases of adult incest survivors. *Johnson v. Johnson,* 701 F. Supp. 1363, 1370 (N.D. Ill. 1988). Michigan courts, in *Meiers-Post v. Schafer*, 427 N.W.2d 606 (Mich. App. 1998) and

*Nicollete v. Carey*, 751 F. Supp. 695 (W.D. Mich. 1990) allowed the use of the discovery rule with reservations. In *Mary D. v. John D.*, 264 Cal. Rptr. 633, 634 (Ct. App. 1990), the California Court of Appeals allowed the discovery rule to be invoked. Washington State enacted the first *statute* to apply the discovery doctrine to civil cases of childhood sexual abuse in 1989 (courts created the discovery rule before the legislatures began writing it into law).

3. National Center for the Victims of Crimes, *supra* note 1. According to the NCVC, 28 states have a "discovery rule" written into their statutes. These include Alaska, Arkansas, California, Florida, Illinois, Iowa, Kansas, Maine, Massachusetts, Minnesota, Missouri, Montana, Nevada, New Hampshire, New Jersey, New Mexico, North Carolina, Oklahoma, Oregon, Rhode Island, South Carolina, South Dakota, Utah, Vermont, Virginia, Washington, Wisconsin, and Wyoming.

4. *See* (from http://www.smith-lawfirm.com/statutestable.html, last updated 2002) A.R.S. §12-502 (interpreted by Arizona Supreme Court as a discovery rule in *Doe v. Roe*, 955 P.2d 951 (Ariz. 1998) (discovery +2), Ark. Code Ann. §16-56-130(a) (discovery +3), Ca. Civ. Proc. Code 340.1 (majority +8 or discovery +3), Colo.⁻Rev. Stat. Ann. §13-80-103.7 (2001) (majority +6 or discovery +3 as interpreted by *Sailsbery v. Parks*, 983 P.2d 137 (Colo. App. 1999), but suits brought pursuant to the discovery rule are only for claims against the perpetrator, not an employer: *Sandoval v. Archdiocese of Denver*, 8 P.3d 598 (Colo. App. 2000), D.C. Code §12-302 (a)(1) (1995) (majority +3 or limited discovery rule), Fla. Stat. Ann.§95.11(7) (majority +7 or discovery +4), Hawaii common law realization-discovery rule: *Dunlea v. Dappen*, 83 Hawaii 28, 924 P.2d 196 (1996), Illinois Statute §13-202.2(b) (majority or discovery +10), Iowa Code Ann. §614.8A (realization-discovery +4), Kansas K.S.A. §60-523 (majority or realization discovery +3), Kentucky KRS §413.249 (majority or discovery +5), Louisiana common law discovery +1: *Doe v. The Roman Catholic Church*, 656 So.2d 5 (La. 1995); *Senn v. Board of*

*Sup'rs of Louisiana State University Agr. and Mechanical College*, 679 So.2d 575, (La. App. 1996), Massachusetts ALM GL c. 260, §4C, as inserted by St. 1993, c. 307 (majority or realization-discovery +3), Minn. Stat. Ann.§541.073 (2002) (discovery +6 running from majority +1 and capped at age 25), Mo. Rev. Stat. §537.046 (discovery +3), Mont. Code Ann.§27-2-216 (realization discovery +3), Nev. Rev. Stat. Ann. §11.215 (majority or realization-discovery +10), N. H. Rev. Stat. Ann. §508:4, I (1983) (realization-discovery +3), N.J. Stat. Ann.§2A:61B-1 (realization discovery +2), N.M. Stat. Ann. §37-1-30 (realization discovery +3), N.C. Gen. Stat. §1-52(16)(1993)) and general incompetency tolling provision (§1-17(a)(1993)) (removal of incompetency or majority +3) incompetence applied to repressed memory in *Leonard v. England*, 115 N.C. App. 103, 445 S.E.2d 50 (1994), North Dakota common law (discovery +2), Ohio common law (discovery +1), Okla. Stat. Ann. Tit. 12, §95 (majority or discovery +2 through 20 years from 18), Or. Rev. Stat. §12.117 (1995 Rev) (majority +6 or realization discovery +3), R.I. Gen. Laws §9-1-51 (realization discovery +7), S.C. Code Ann. §15-3-555 (majority +6 or realization-discovery +3), S.D. Codified Laws Ann. §26-10-25, et seq. (realization-discovery +3), Tennessee common law (discovery +1), Texas Supreme Court has adopted a case-by-case discovery rule (discovery +5), Utah Code Ann. §78-12-25.1 (majority or discovery +4) , Vt. Stat. Ann. Tit. 12, §522 (discovery +6), Va. Code Ann. §8.01-243 (2003) (realization discovery +2), Wash. Rev. Code Ann. §4.16.340 (majority or realization-discovery +3), W. Va. Code §55-2-15 (majority or discovery +2 capped at 20 from the date of the act), Wis. Stat. Ann. §893.587 , 893.16 (1) (minority tolling)(2002) (majority or realization-discovery +5), Wyo. Stat. §1-3-105 (majority +8 or realization-discovery +3).

5. http://voicefromthedesert.blogspot.com/2007/05/whatever-you-dosol-reform-resource.html (includes excerpts from psychologists' accounts of the effects on victims, including O'Dea); Mark Sauer, *Experts Say Long Delays in Reporting Sexual Abuse Are Common; Most Victims Don't Come Forward at All*, UNION

TRIBUNE (San Diego), June 3, 2007, *available at* http://www.
signonsandiego.com/news/metro/20070603–9999–1m3victims.
html.

6. David R. Price & James J. McDonald, Jr., *The Problem of False
Claims of Clergy Sexual Abuse (Catholic Church Copes with Lawsuits over Sexual Abuse)*, RISK MANAGEMENT, Jan. 1, 2003, at 48,
50. ("While documented cases of clergy sexual abuse are tragic
and deserving of compensation, all claims nonetheless require
scrutiny. False, fabricated and exaggerated claims do occur. Even
if such claims are ultimately defeated, though, the defense costs
can be substantial and the damage to those falsely accused can be
permanent. Risk managers or claims administrators faced with
a claim of clergy sexual abuse should consider whether the claim
might be false, and whether such could be proven in court. By
applying techniques proven effective in the defense of other types
of claims of sexual misconduct, false, fabricated or exaggerated
claims of abuse may be exposed.")

## 3. The Solution Is Clear and Simple

1. *See, e.g.*, Marci Hamilton, *States Move to Enact Laws Allowing
the Death Penalty for Pedophiles*, FINDLAW.COM, May 31, 2007,
http://writ.news.FindLaw.com/hamilton/20070531.html.

2. Some states that use this practice: Pennsylvania, New Jersey,
Florida; Massachusetts (in Massachusetts there are exclusion
zones for a particular offender under the terms of their parole
that may include for example the victim's neighborhood (ALM
GL ch. 127, §133D1/2 (2007)); Georgia (O.C.G.A. §42-1-15);
Kentucky (KRS §17.545); Michigan (M.C.L.A. 28.734–735(2007));
Ohio (O.H. S.T. §2950.034(2007)); Tennessee (Tenn. Code Ann.)
§40-39-211 (2007)); Idaho (Idaho Code §18-8329)(2007)); Indiana
(Burns Ind. Code Ann. §35-38-2-2.2 (2007)); Nevada (Nev. Rev.
Stat. Ann. §176A.410 (2007)); Wisconsin (Wisconsin (Wis. Stat.
§301.48 (3)(c)). For each person who is subject to global posi-
tioning system tracking under this section, the department shall

create individualized exclusion and inclusion zones for the person, if necessary to protect public safety).

3. *See, e.g.,* California's database: http://www.meganslaw.ca.gov/Search.aspx?lang=ENGLISH.

4. *Where on Earth Are Sex Offenders?*, 32 STATE LEGISLATURES MAGAZINE 14 (March 2006).

5. PA 07-143, *An Act Concerning Jessica's Law and Consensual Sexual Acts Between Adolescents Close in Age to Each Other* (effective 7/1/07).

6. Death Penalty Information Center, http://www.deathpenaltyinfo.org/article.php?did=2184.

7. Adam Liptak, *Death Penalty in Some Cases of Child Sex Is Widening*, N.Y. TIMES, June 10, 2006, at A9.

8. Brad Kellar, *Governor Signs Jessica's Law, Bill Authored by Deuell*, HERALD BANNER, July 18, 2007, *available at* http://www.heraldbanner.com/local_story_199012834.html.

9. Associated Press, *South Carolina Senate Passes Death Penalty for Repeat Child Rapists*, Mar. 28, 2006, *available at* http://www.foxnews.com/story/0,2933,189423,00.html.

10. *See Kansas v. Hendricks*, 521 U.S. 346 (1997).

11. Barbara Bryant, *Sex-Offender Commitments Hit Legal Roadblock in N.Y.*, 42 PSYCHIATRIC NEWS 17 (Feb. 2, 2007), *available at* http://pn.psychiatryonline.org/cgi/content/full/42/3/17.

12. Anemona Hartocollis, *Sex Offenders Held Illegally, Judge Rules*, N.Y. TIMES, Nov. 16, 2005, *available at* http://www.nytimes.com/2005/11/16/nyregion/16ruling.html?ex=1183176000&en=d8be5e44fe31775d&ei=5070.

13. Bryant, *supra* note 11.

14. Erik Borgsteede, *Sex Offender Law Would Use GPS*, THE DAILY TAR HEEL (Chapel Hill, N.C.), June 21, 2007, *available at* http://media.www.dailytarheel.com/media/storage/paper885/news/2007/06/21/StateNational/Sex-Offender.Law.Would.Use.Gps-2916964.shtml.

15. Alabama (Ala. Code §15-20-26.1); California (Cal. Pen. Code §3004(2007)), Colorado (C.R.S. 18-1.3-204 (2006)), Connecticut (Conn. Gen. Stat. §53a-30 (2007)), Florida (Fl. Stat. §947.1405

(2007)), Georgia (O.C.G.A. §42-1-14), Hawaii (H.R.S. §706-624 (2007)), Illinois (§730 ILCS 5/3–3–7 (2007)), Iowa (I.C.A. §692A.4A (2007)), Kansas (K.S.A. §22-3717 (2006)), Louisiana (La. R.S. 15:550 (2007) (pilot program)); Maine (17-A M.R.S. §1231 (2007)), Massachusetts (ALM GL ch. 127, §133D1/2 (2007)/ ALM GL ch. 265, §47 (2007)), Michigan (MCLS §750.520n (2007)), Mississippi (Miss. Code Ann. §99-19-84 (2007)), Missouri (§217.735 R.S.Mo. (2007)), Nebraska (R.R.S. Neb. §83-174.03 (2007)), New Jersey (N.J. Stat. §30:4-123.83 (2007)), North Carolina (N.C. Gen. Stat. §14-208.40 (2007)) (establishing a program), North Dakota (N.D. Cent. Code, §12-67-02 (2007)), Ohio (ORC Ann. 2929.13 (2007)), Oklahoma (57 Okl. St. §510.9 (2007)), Rhode Island (R.I. Gen. Laws §11-37-8.2.1 (2007)), South Carolina (S.C. Code Ann. §23-3-540 (2006)), Tennessee (T.C.A. 40–39–303), Texas (Tex. Health & Safety Code §841.082 (2007)), Virginia (Va. Code Ann. §19.2-303 (2007)), Washington (Rev. Code Wash. (ARCW) §9.94A.715 (2007)), West Virginia (W. Va. Code §62-11D-3 (2007)), Wisconsin (Wis. Stat. §301.48 (2006)).

16. Township of Hamilton, NJ Code of Ordinances Sec. 86–20. Sex offender residency prohibition; 2,500 feet. (Ord. No. 05–017, 5–17–2005) available at: http://www.municode.com/Resources/gateway. asp?pid=12709&sid=30.

17. Marci Hamilton, *The Drive to Create Pedophile-Free Zones: Why It Won't Work – And What Will Work*, FINDLAW.COM, Aug. 25, 2005, http://writ.news.FindLaw.com/hamilton/20050825.html.

18. *See, e.g.*, 23 Pa.C.S. §6311 (Mandatory reporters include, but are not limited to: any licensed physician, osteopath, medical examiner, coroner, funeral director, dentist, optometrist, chiropractor, podiatrist, intern, registered nurse, licensed practical nurse, hospital personnel engaged in the admission, examination, care or treatment of persons, Christian Science practitioner, member of the clergy, school administrator, school teacher, school nurse, social services worker, day care center worker or any other child care or foster care worker, mental health professional, peace officer, or law enforcement official.) And background checks are required of school employees under 23 Pa.C.S.

§6355. *See also* Susan K. Smith, Mandatory Reporting of Child Abuse and Neglect, http://www.smith-lawfirm.com/mandatory_reporting.htm (last edited Nov. 2, 2006) (this site lists the statute on mandatory reporting for each state). Other states also requiring background checks of school employees include Alaska (Alaska Stat. §14.20.015 (2007)); Alabama (Code of Ala. §16-22A-5 (2007)); Arkansas (Ark. Stat. Ann. §6-17-410-414 (2007), A.C.A. §20-78-601-604 (2007) (child care providers)); California (Cal Ed Code §44274.2, §44332.6 (2007) (teacher certificates)); Connecticut (Conn. Gen. Stat. §10-221d (2007)); Delaware (11 Del. C. §8571 (2007) (public school employees)); Georgia (O.C.G.A. §20-1A-32 (2007) (early child care facilities)); Idaho (Idaho Code §33-130 (2007)); Indiana (Burns Ind. Code Ann. §20-26-5-10 (2007) (discretionary)); Kansas (KRS §160.380 (2006) (public-mandatory), KRS §160.151 (2006) (private-discretionary), KRS §164.28 (2006) (public postsecondary mandatory)); Mississippi (Miss. Code Ann. §37-9-17 (2007)); Missouri (§168.133 R.S.Mo. (2007)); New Jersey (N.J. Stat. §30:5B-6.13 (2007) (child care services employees)); New Mexico (N.M. Stat. Ann. §22-10A-5 (2007)); Pennsylvania (24 P.S. §1-111 (2006)); Tennessee (Tenn. Code Ann. §71-3-507 (2007) (child service providers)); Rhode Island (R.I. Gen. Laws §16-2-18.1 (2007), R.I. Gen. Laws §16-48.1-3 (2007) (very young children)); South Dakota (S.D. Codified Laws §13-10-12 (2007)); Utah (Utah Code Ann. §53A-1a-512.5 (2007)); Wyoming (Wyo. Stat. §21-2-802 (2007)).

19. C.R.S. §§19-3-304. The complete list includes physicians or surgeons, including a physician in training; child health associates; medical examiners or coroners; dentists; osteopaths; optometrists; chiropractors; chiropodists or podiatrists; registered nurses or licensed practical nurse; hospital personnel engaged in the admission, care, or treatment of patients; Christian Science practitioners; public or private school officials or employees; social workers or workers in any facility or agency that is licensed or certified under; mental health professionals; dental hygienists; psychologists; physical therapists; veterinarians; peace officers; pharmacists; commercial film and photographic print processors;

firefighters; victim's advocates; licensed professional counselors; licensed marriage and family therapists; unlicensed psychotherapists; clergy members; registered dietitians; juvenile parole and probation officers; child and family investigators; and officers and agents of the state bureau of animal protection and animal control officers.

20. FRAWLEY-O'DEA, *supra* note 2, ch. 1 (Priests removed from the ministry are likely to reoffend); *id.* at 179 (citing the John Jay Study) ("[f]ew priests sexually abuse their victims only one time... This finding argues against constructing sexual abuse by a priest as a momentary lapse of judgment but rather presses for viewing the perpetrator as dangerously likely to reabuse a young person many times."); *see also* KENNETH V. LANNING, CHILD MOLESTERS: A BEHAVIORAL ANALYSIS 50, 58 (4th ed. 2001). (Many perpetrators have multiple victims and prior arrests for abuse.)

21. Kristen Lombardi, *Geoghan: Convicted at Last*, BOSTON PHOENIX, Jan. 24–31, 2002, *available at* http://bostonphoenix.com/boston/news_features/other_stories/multipage/documents/02127282.htm.

22. Kathleen Burge, *In Reversal, Judge Reinstates Child Rape Charges Against Geoghan*, BOSTON GLOBE, Aug. 30, 2002, *available at* http://boston.com/globe/spotlight/abuse/stories3/083002_geoghan.htm.

23. E-mail from Matt Conaty, to Karen Peterson and Deborah Hudson, Delaware State legislators (Jun. 19, 2007, 12:26:48 EST) (on file with author) (forwarded child sexual abuse survivor's thank you for the Delaware SOL reform).

24. Julian Emerson, *Painful Memories: Former Rice Lake Pastor Faces Sex Abuse Charges*, LEADER-TELEGRAM ONLINE (Eau Claire, Wis.), May 20, 2007 (on file with author).

25. Associated Press, *Former Catholic Priest Michael Wempe Free While Awaiting Trial*, Aug. 17, 2004, *available at* http://www.bishop-accountability.org/news2004_07_12/2004_08_17_AP_FormerCatholic.htm.

26. John Spano, *Ex-Priest Gets 10 Years in Church Sex Abuse Scandal*, L.A. TIMES, Dec. 4, 2007, at 1; Associated Press, *Prosecutor: Child Victims Drawn to Priest*, Jan. 24, 2006, *available at* http://www.

cbsnews.com/stories/2006/01/24/ap/national/mainD8FAOMC00. shtml; *Pickets to Target Paroled Pedophile's Home*, L.A. TIMES, Jun. 9, 2007, at 4.

27. Jessica Garrison, *Ex-Priest to Face More Charges, Prosecutor Says: The Molestation Accusations against Michael Baker Involve a Second Alleged Victim*, L.A. TIMES, Dec. 13, 2006, at B10 ("Two sources said separately on condition of anonymity that investigators had been led to the second alleged victim in part through information from Baker's personnel file. The Los Angeles Archdiocese had vigorously fought turning over the personnel files to prosecutors, going all the way to the U.S. Supreme Court before losing that fight in April. The archdiocese turned over the files soon after").

28. Emerson, *supra* note 24. ("Toro wasn't only interested in him, Guillen said. The pastor also attempted to convince Guillen's younger brother, 10-year-old Nelson, to come to work for him at the church, but Guillen intervened. 'After what happened to me, there was no way I was going to let him be with my brother,' Guillen said."); *see also* E-mail from Warren Land, to Marci A. Hamilton (Apr. 27, 2007, 22:20:58 EST) (on file with author) ("Dear Ms. Hamilton, it feels very good to write you. I am 39 years old, and until recently lived silently with the pain of having been molested. My molestation was sexual; and occurred, I believe, at the age of 12 (perhaps 13). I live in New Jersey, and the abuse occurred in Pennsylvania. The predator was a lay person employed as a teacher at the Catholic grade school where I was a student. My father at the time was dying of a brain tumor. I am a physician. I have a failing marriage. Very recently I decided to speak up. Tragically, *my brother is a victim of the same person* (a convicted child molester). We have been in contact with the police, and DA's office. Our main concern is the statute of limitation in Pennsylvania. We believe it was extended recently to the age of 50, but it is not retroactive. Therefore, we may not be able to proceed criminally. The DA's office, however, has told us we can still file criminal charges. What do you think about this? Thank you! – Warren Land").

29. Kieran Crowley, *Family's Hell: Priest Molested All Five Kids, $25m Suit Says*, NEW YORK POST, Jan. 12, 2006, *available at* http://www.bishop-accountability.org/news3/2006_01_12_Crowley_FamilysHell_Daniel_Babis.htm; Eden Laikin, *Siblings Sue RVC Diocese, Bishop William Murphy*, NEWSDAY, Jan. 12, 2006, *available at* http://www.newsday.com/news/local/longisland/ny-liabus0112,0,5847824.story.

30. Ashbel S. Green, *Secrets of a Small Town Priest: Priest Suit Reveals Brothers' Secret*, OregonianLive.com, June 30, 2002, http://www.oregonlive.com/special/priest/index.ssf?/special/oregonian/priest/020630.html.

31. http://www.bishop-accountability.org/news2006/ 01_02/2006_01_12_Herzog_LawsuitClaims.htm; http://www.bishop-accountability.org/news2006/01_02/2006_01_12_Gustafson_6Allege.htm.

32. Gar Joseph, *Clout: Sexcapade at Convention Center?*, PHILADEL-PHIA DAILY NEWS, June 22, 2007, *available at* http://www.philly.com/dailynews/columnists/clout/20070622_Clout___Sexcapade_at_Convention_Center_.html.

33. *Id.*

## 4. What It Will Take to Protect Children

1. ALA. CODE §15-3-5 (2007).

2. Terry Carter, "Collaring the Clergy," ABA JOURNAL, June 4, 2007, *available at* http://www.abanet.org/journal/redesign/06fand.html.

3. *Stogner v. California*, 539 U.S. 607 (2003).

4. Jean Guccione, *Void of '03 Abuse Law Sought*, L.A. TIMES, Sept. 9, 2005, *available at* http://www.bishop-accountability.org/news2005_07_12/2005_09_09_Guccione_VoidOf.htm.

5. 72 Am Jur 2d, States, Territories, and Dependencies, §99 General Rule as to State's Immunity from Suit, at 490.

6. LANNING, *supra* note 20, ch. 3.

7. 18 U.S.C. §3283 (2007).

8. *Id.*

9. *South Dakota v. Dole*, 483 U.S. 203 (1987).

10. *Jackson v. Birmingham Bd. of Educ.*, 544 U.S. 167, 181–182 (2005).
11. 42 U.S.C. §16942 (2007).
12. 42 U.S.C. §16983 (2007).
13. 42 U.S.C. §16987 (2007).
14. 42 U.S.C. §16985 (2007).
15. 42 U.S.C. §280c-6 (2007).
16. 42 U.S.C. §290bb-25 (2007).
17. 42 U.S.C. §621 (2007).
18. 42 U.S.C. §629h (2007).
19. 42 U.S.C. §629i (2007).
20. 42 U.S.C. §5116 (2007).
21. 42 U.S.C. §10420 (2007).
22. 42 U.S.C. §10603 (2007).
23. 42 U.S.C. §13971 (2007).

## 5. Barrier #1: The Insurance Industry

1. deeplyblasphemous.blogspot.com.
2. Michael J. Bemi, *TNCRRG Provides Series of Legal Defense Practice Workshops: Workshops Specifically Address the Handling of Claims Related to Sexual Misconduct*, VIRTUS ONLINE, http://www.virtus.org/virtus/newsletter.cfm?newsletter_id=37.
3. Jean Torkelson, *Sex Abuse Bill in Doubt: House Soundly Rejects Compromise in Favor of Original*, ROCKY MOUNTAIN NEWS (Denver, Co.), May 5, 2006, *available at* http://www.rockymountainnews.com/drmn/government/article/0,2777,DRMN_23906_4675655,00.html.
4. *Id.*
5. Insurance Institute of Indiana, Legislative Successes, http://www.insuranceinstitute.org/interested.html.
6. Opensecrets.org, Lobbying Spending Database, http://www.opensecrets.org/lobbyists (follow "Top Industries" hyperlink; then follow "2006" dropdown).
7. Swivel.com, Lobbying – Top Spending Sectors, Year-Over-Year, http://www.swivel.com/data_sets/show/1002568.

8. Chris McGann, *Lobbying Is Big Business in State*, SEATTLE POST-INTELLIGENCER, July 1, 2007, *available at* http://seattlepi.nwsource.com/local/322060_lobbyists02.html.

9. Bizstats.com, Size of U.S. Markets by Industry 2007, http://www.bizstats.com/marketsizes.htm.

10. April M. Washington & Todd Hartman, *Bill Nears End of the Road: 'A Lot Lost' As Vote Likely on Monday, Fitz-Gerald Says*, ROCKY MOUNTAIN NEWS (Denver, Co.), May 6, 2006, *available at* http://www.rockymountainnews.com/drmn/government/article/0,2777,DRMN_23906_4678866,00.html. (Sen. Joan Fitz-Gerald said she didn't sleep a wink Thursday night . . . Her proposal died Thursday afternoon . . . HB 1090's path has been complex. Two powerful institutions – the Colorado Catholic Conference and the insurance industry – have worked behind-the-scenes to weaken it and limit their liability to suits).

11. Tom Beyerlein, *Candidate to Push for Abuse Victims' Day in Court*, DAYTON DAILY NEWS, Apr. 6, 2006, *available at* http://www.daytondailynews.com/localnews/content/localnews/daily/0406priest.html.

12. Marci Hamilton, Children, Churches, and the Law: Massachusetts' Proposal to Require Clergy to Report Child Abuse, FINDLAW.COM, Aug. 16, 2001, http://writ.news.FindLaw.com/hamilton/20010816.html.

13. Jim Siegel & Dennis M. Mahoney, *Silence Shattered on Sex Abuse*, THE COLUMBUS DISPATCH, Jan. 12, 2006, *available at* http://www.columbusdispatch.com/news-story.php?story=dispatch/2006/01/12/20060112-A1–01.html.

14. Catherine Candisky & Jim Siegel, *Abusive Priests Get Legal Break: House Won't Allow Lawsuits To Go Back 35 Years*, COLUMBUS DISPATCH, March 29, 2006, *available at* http://www.bishop-accountability.org/news2006/03_04/2006_03_29_Candisky_AbusivePriests.html.

15. *See* http://www.bishop-accountability.org/pa_philadelphia/Philly_GJ_report.htm for the text of the report and news and commentary about the report.

16. Dave Janoski, *Bill Aims to Loosen Limits on Suits*, TIMES LEADER (Wilkes-Barre, Pa.), July 9, 2006, at A1.

17. Martha Raffaele, *House Weighs How to Help Victims Abused by Priests*, THE MORNING CALL (Harrisburg, Pa.), Dec. 7, 2005, *available at* http://www.bishop-accountability.org/news2005_07_12/2005_12_07_Raffaele_HouseWeighs.htm. The first Pennsylvania civil window bill (HB 2300) was introduced Dec. 6, 2005, by Rep. Reichley. He reintroduced it in 2007. *See* http://www.legis.state.pa.us/cfdocs/billinfo/billinfo.cfm?syear=2007&sind=0&body=H&type=B&BN=1574.

18. *See, e.g.,* John Nolan, *Clergy-abuse Compensation Panel Distributes $3.2 Million*, BEACON JOURNAL (Akron, Ohio) Mar. 9, 2005, *available at* http://bishop-accountability.org/abuse2005archives/009882.html.

19. Beth Miller, *Child Sex Abuse Victims May Get More Time to Sue*, THE NEWS JOURNAL (Wilmington, Del.), May 30, 2006, at 1B.

20. Beth Miller, *Senate Committee Releases Bill to Facilitate Sexual Abuse Victims*, THE NEWS JOURNAL (Wilmington, Del.), May 30, 2007, at B2.

21. *Id.*

22. *Id.*

23. Beth Miller, *Child Sex-Abuse Victims Cheer Law*, THE NEWS JOURNAL (Wilmington, Del.), July 11, 2007, *available at* http://www.delawareonline.com/apps/pbcs.dll/article?AID=/20070711/NEWS/707110342/1006.

## 6. Barrier #2: The Hierarchy of the Roman Catholic Church

1. *See* The *Boston Globe* Spotlight Investigation: Abuse in the Catholic Church, at http://www.boston.com/globe/spotlight/abuse/.

2. http://www.cara.georgetown.edu/bulletin/index.htm (this data is current as of 2006).

3. The federal government employed 2,700,392 civilian personnel as of September 2006. *See* http://www.opm.gov/feddata/html/2006/september/table1.asp.

4. http://money.cnn.com/magazines/fortune/fortune500/performers/ companies/by_employees/index.html (this data is current as of 2005).

5. Central Statistics Office (2007). Statistical Yearbook of the Church 2005. Libreria Editrice Vaticana.

6. http://www.cara.georgetown.edu/bulletin/index.htm (this data is current as of 2006).

7. Ralph Blumenthal, *Citing Abuses, Texas Governor Ousts Leader of Youth Agency*, NEW YORK TIMES, Mar. 1, 2007, at A14. According to the TYC Web site, the residential end-of-year population for 2006 was 4800. *See* http://www.tyc.state.tx.us/research/growth_ charts.html. It appears from the Web site that there are fifteen institutions and nine halfway houses operated by the TYC. *See* http://www.tyc.state.tx.us/programs/facility_address.html.

8. http://www.dallasnews.com/investigativereports/tyc//.

9. *See, e.g., Doe ex rel. Doe v. Dallas Indep. Sch. Dist.*, 220 F.3d 380 (5th Cir. 2000); *Lourim v. Swensen*, 977 P.2d 1157 (Or. 1999); *Snyder v. Boy Scouts of America, Inc.*, 253 Cal. Rptr. 156 (Cal. Ct. App. 1988); *see also Idaho's 'Post Register' Uncovers Pedophiles Among Boy Scout Officials*, Associated Press (Idaho Falls), July 5, 2005, *available at* http://www.editorandpublisher.com/eandp/ news/article_display.jsp?vnu_content_id=1000973214.

10. David Edwards & Muriel Kane, *CBS: 5,100 Boy Scout leaders removed for abuse*, Aug. 29, 2007, *available at* http:// rawstory.com/news/2007/CBS_5100_Boy_Scout_leaders_removed_ 0829.html.

11. *Southern Baptists urged to root out molesters: advocates for sex abuse victims in Roman Catholic Church shift their focus*, Associated Press (Nashville, TN), Feb. 22, 2007, *available at* http://www.msnbc.msn.com/id/17265721/.

12. *See* Marci A. Hamilton, *How the Ohio Legislature Betrayed Child Victims of Clergy Abuse, and How We Can Stop It from Happening Nationwide*, FINDLAW.COM, Apr. 6, 2006, http://writ. news.FindLaw.com/hamilton/20060406.html.

13. Presbyterian USA. *See* http://www.pcusa.org/gapjc/misconduct. htm.

14. *See* http://www.wfn.org/2002/05/msg00245.html; http://findarticles.com/p/articles/mi_qn4155/is_20020515/ai_n12464867.

15. David O'Reilly, *D.A. Promotes Sex-Abuse Bill*, PHILADELPHIA INQUIRER, Oct. 14, 2006, *available at* http://www.bishop-accountability.org/news2006/09_10/2006_10_14_OReilly_DAPromotes.htm.

16. Jay Tokasz, *Diocese Hardly Touched by Sex Suits; Statute of Limitations Cited as Main Reason*, BUFFALO NEWS, July 22, 2007, at A1.

17. Associated Press, *An Explanation of the Clergy Abuse Litigation in California*, Oct. 9, 2004, *available at* http://www.snapnetwork.org/legal_courts/stories/ca_explanation_calif_cases.htm. California case breakdown by region: Clergy I covers 556 cases against the Archdiocese of Los Angeles and the Diocese of Orange; together, the dioceses have more than 4.6 million parishioners. Clergy II covers 140 cases from the Diocese of San Diego and the Diocese of San Bernardino; together, the dioceses have about 2 million parishioners. Clergy III covers 160 cases from the dioceses of San Francisco, Sacramento, Stockton, Fresno, Santa Rosa, Monterey, San Jose, and Oakland.

18. S.B. 1779, Damages: Childhood Sexual Abuse: Statute of Limitations. An Act to Amend Section 340.1 of the Code of Civil Procedure (Ca. 2002), *available at* http://www.legislature.ca.gov/port-statute.html.

19. *In re The Roman Catholic Bishop of San Diego*, No. 07cv1355-IEG-(RBB), 2007 U.S. Dist. LEXIS 60954, at *6 (S.D. Cal. Aug. 20, 2007).

20. Marci Hamilton, Op-Ed., *A "Window" for Victims of Abuse*, L.A. TIMES, July 19, 2007, at A23.

21. Jean Guccione & William Lobdell, *Law Spurred Flood of Sex Abuse Suits: Hundreds Filed Claims in One-Year Window for Old Cases, Up to 800 People Target Dioceses in State*, L.A. TIMES, Jan. 1, 2004, at A1.

"The whole notion that the law was created for the Catholic Church – while that may be true, it has much wider consequences," said Newport Beach attorney Mark Kelegian, who has filed two dozen cases against religious organizations and community groups, including the Boys Scouts of America.

Other lawsuits name a variety of defendants, including the Explorers, the Salvation Army and the Seventh-day Adventist Church.

Five men, for example, have accused two male teachers at Monterey Bay Academy, an Adventist boarding school in La Selva Beach, of giving them alcohol and marijuana when they were teenagers, then raping them, according to their lawyer Joseph P. Scully.

And three lawsuits allege that Deputy Chief David Kalish of the Los Angeles Police Department molested three teenage boys more than 20 years ago when they were Explorers. Kalish, who has denied the charges, has been on paid leave since March, when the allegations became public. No criminal charges will be filed.

22. Peter Wilkinson, *The Life and Death of the Chosen One*, ROLLING STONE, June 30, 2005. *See also* http://www.xfamily. org/index.php/Category:Places; http://www.xfamily.org/index. php/Statistics (describing locations).
23. Wilkinson, *supra* note 22, at 121.
24. *Id.* at 121–122.
25. *Id.*
26. *Melanie H. v. Sisters of Precious Blood*, No. 04-1596-WQH-(WMc), slip op. at 10–11, (S.D. Cal. 2005).
27. Martha Bellisle, *Lawmaker Wants to Give Abuse Victims Time to Sue*, RENO GAZETTE-JOURNAL, Aug. 19, 2007, *available at* http://news.rgj.com/apps/pbcs.dll/article?AID=/20070819/NEWS/ 708190346/1321/NEWS.
28. *Id.*
29. Laurie Goodstein, *After Abuse Settlement, an Apology to Victims*, N.Y. TIMES, July 16, 2007, at A9.
30. Angelica Martinez & Karen Kucher, *San Diego Priest Abuse Claims Settled*, UNION-TRIBUNE (San Diego), Sep. 7,

2007, *available at* http://www.signonsandiego.com/news/metro/20070907–1449-bn07diocese3.html.

31. Marci A. Hamilton, *The Long and Difficult Road to Protecting Children from Sexual Abuse: A Tale of Three States, and How They Revised Their Statutes*, FINDLAW.COM, May 19, 2005, http://writ.corporate.FindLaw.com/hamilton/20050519.html.

32. TWIST OF FAITH (HBO Documentary 2004) http://www.hbo.com/docs/programs/twistoffaith/index.html.

33. Ohio Legislative Service Commission, Senate Bills – Status Report of Legislation, 126 General Assembly, SB 17, *available at* http://lsc.state.oh.us/coderev/sen126.nsf/Senate+Bill+Number/0017?OpenDocument.

34. E-mail from Daniel Frondorf, Co-Director of SNAP Cincinnati to Marci Hamilton, Author (Aug. 2, 2007, 01:46:13) (on file with author).

35. Bill Frogameni, *Victims, Church Battle over Bill*, NATIONAL CATHOLIC REPORTER, Dec. 9, 2005, *available at* http://NCRonline.com.

36. Jim Provence, *Church Proposes Molestation Registry: Catholic Officials Oppose Lifting Time Limit on Sex-Abuse Lawsuits*, TOLEDO BLADE, Dec. 26, 2005, *available at* http://www.toledoblade.com/apps/pbcs.dll/article?AID=/20051226/NEWS08/512260307/-1/NEWS.

37. Julie Carr Smyth, *Dozens Speak in Support of Ohio's Priest-Abuse Bill*, PLAIN DEALER (Cleveland), Dec. 9, 2005, at B5.

38. Editorial, *The Bishops Stone Wall*, TOLEDO BLADE, Dec. 21, 2005.

39. Jim Siegel, *Sponsor of Priest-Abuse Bill Wants Church to Let It Pass*, COLUMBUS DISPATCH, Nov. 10, 2005, at 1E (emphasis added).

40. Frogameni, *supra* note 35.

41. Smyth, *supra* note 37.

42. Testimony of Bishop Thomas Gumbleton, delivered to the Judiciary Committee, Ohio House of Representatives, January 2006, *available at* http://www.votf.org/Press/pressrelease/testimony0106.html.

43. Provence, *supra* note 36.

44. Catherine Candisky & Jim Siegel, *Abusive Priests Get Legal Break: House Won't Allow Lawsuits To Go Back 35 Years*, COLUMBUS DISPATCH, Mar. 29, 2006, at A1.

45. Jim Provence, *Ohio Legislature: Window Closed for Old Abuse Charges, Bill Adds Registry, Tells Clergy to Report Cases*, TOLEDO BLADE, Mar. 30, 2006.

46. Archdiocese of Denver, http://www.archden.org/archbishop-s-biography/archbishops-biography.html.

47. Power, *supra* note 31.

48. Eric Gorski, *Lawsuit Will Claim Church Coverup: The Complaint against the Archdiocese of Denver Is the First since Accusations against an Ex-Priest Surfaced Last Month*, DENVER POST, Aug. 18, 2005, at A1.

49. *Id.*

50. Jean Torkelson, *Judge Clears Path for Sex Abuse Lawsuits*, ROCKY MOUNTAIN NEWS (Denver, Co.), Mar. 28, 2007, *available at* http://reform-network.net/?m=20070328.

51. Mark P. Couch and Eric Gorski, *Catholic Conference Hires Lobbyist on Abuse Bills: The Firm That Was Chosen Has Ties to Gov. Owens but Says That Relationship Won't Affect Its Work on Church Issues*, DENVER POST, Mar. 8, 2006, at B1. Phase Line Strategies LLC, http://www.phaseline.com/clients.htm.

52. Catholic News Agency, *Colorado Bishops Blast Limitation Lifting Legislation*, Feb. 1, 2006, *available at* http://www.catholic.org/national/national_story.php?id=18547.

53. Mary DeTurris Poust, *Church in Colorado Seeks Fair Treatment Under Law*, OUR SUNDAY VISITOR, Mar. 5, 2005, *available at* http://www.bishopaccountability.org.

54. Joe Feuerherd, *Church Lobbyists Battle to Limit Abuse Suits: More Than A Dozen States Consider Lifting Statutes of Limitations*, NATIONAL CATHOLIC REPORTER, Mar. 31, 2006, *available at* http://ncronline.org/NCR_Online/archives2/2006a/033106/033106a.php.

55. David O'Reilly, *Bishops: We're Not Blocking Legislation; The Catholic Church Said Its Passive Approach on Pa. Sex-Abuse Bills Did Not Indicate Opposition*, PHILADELPHIA INQUIRER,

Aug. 14, 2006, *available at* http://www.philly.com/mld/inquirer/living/religion/15267576.htm.

56. *Id.*

57. Jim Spencer, *Foes Wrap Sex-Abuse Bill in Distortions*, DENVER POST, Apr. 28 2006, at B1.

58. *See* Marci Hamilton, *How the Laws Look the Other Way When It Comes to the Financial Improprieties of Religious Institutions, and How They Should Be Amended to Make Them Accountable*, FINDLAW.COM, May 4, 2006, http://writ.lp.FindLaw.com/hamilton/20060504.html. *See also* Stephanie Ebbert, *Diocese Property Deals Net $90m*, BOSTON GLOBE, Nov. 6, 2005, at A1 (details the church's liquidation of property, but church denies that liquidation is for capital); Paul Pringle and Ted Rohrlich, *Scandal Could Prompt Church to Sell Property*, L.A. TIMES, Dec. 3, 2006, *available at* http://www.latimes.com/news/local/la-me-money3dec03,0,5843035.story?coll=la-home-headlines (Cardinal O'Malley explaining the trend and discussing church assets).

59. Charity Choices, http://www.charitablechoices.org/charities/CaCharYout/questions.asp. ("Catholic Charities CYO obtains approximately 80 percent of its annual operating budget through government funding sources.")

60. Editorial, *Disappearing Parishes*, BOSTON GLOBE, May 26, 2004, *available at* http://www.boston.com/news/globe/editorial_opinion/editorials/articles/2004/05/26/disappearing_parishes.

61. Feuerherd, *supra* note 54.

62. Mike McPhee, *Sex-Abuse Suits Proceed: Bills Demise Irrelevant, Lawyers Say the Lawsuits against the Catholic Church Will Have to Go Around the Current Statute of Limitations*, DENVER POST, May 6, 2006, *available at* http://www.denverpost.com/news/ci_3791309.

63. Press Release, State of Delaware, Governor Minner Signs Senate Bill 29, July 10, 2007, *available at* http://governor.delaware.gov/071007sb29billsigning.shtml#TopOfPage.

64. Beth Miller, *Abused Children May Get More Time to Sue; Bill Would Increase Statute of Limitations to Six Years from Two*, NEWS JOURNAL (Wilmington, Del.), May 30, 2006, at B1.

65. Testimony of Thomas Doyle, J.C.D., C.A.D.C., In Support of S.B. 29, State Law of Delaware, Dover, Delaware, April 4, 2007, *available at* http://www.bishop-accountability.org/news2007/05_06/2007_05_04_VoicefromtheDesert_TomDoyle.htm.

66. Beth Miller, *Senate Committee Releases Bill on Sexual Abuse Suits*, NEWS JOURNAL (Wilmington, Del.), May 30, 2007, at B2.

67. Child Victims Voice, http//www.childvictimsvoice.com/supports.html.

68. Beth Miller, *Limits on Sex Abuse Suits Set for Debate*, NEWS JOURNAL (Wilmington, Del.), June 18, 2007, at A1.

69. Beth Miller, *Child Sex-Abuse Victims Cheer Law*, NEWS JOURNAL (Wilmington, Del.), July 11, 2007, at B1.

70. *Id.*

71. *Id.*

72. *Id.*

## 7. The Other Barriers

1. Associated Press, *Abuse Is No. 1 Reason Teachers Lose Licenses in W. Va.*, HERALD-MAIL (W. Va.), Oct. 17, 2005, *available at* http://www.bishop-accountability.org/news2005_07_12/2005_10_17_AP_AbuseIs.htm.

2. Eric Gorski, *Church Sways Sex-Abuse Bills*, DENVER POST, Feb. 12, 2006, at C1.

3. *Brouillet v. Cowles Publ'g Co.*, 791 P.2d 526, 532 (Wash. 1990) ("Sexual abuse of students is a proper matter of public concern...Because the information sought is of legitimate public interest, we conclude that no privacy right has been violated."); *Clergy Cases I & III*, Case nos. JCCP 4286, 4359-PDL (Cal. Super. Ct. 2007); *see also* John Spano & Greg Krikorian, *Judge Allows Release of Clergy Personnel Files; The Ruling States that Protecting Children from Abuse Outweighs a Priest's Right to Privacy*, L.A. TIMES, June 19, 2007, at B1.

4. Maureen O'Hagan & Christine Williams, *Union, District Joined Forces to Block Records*, SEATTLE TIMES, Dec. 14, 2003, at A21.

5. *See, e.g., Bellevue John Does v. Bellevue Sch. Dist. No. 405*, 120 P.3d 616 (Wash. Ct. App. 2005), *reh'g granted* (2007).

6. T. R. Reid, *Catholic Leaders Fight Legislation on Suits; States Consider Easing Statutes of Limitations*, WASH. POST, Apr. 1, 2006, at A10.

7. *See* Associated Press, *supra* note 1.

8. *Id.*

9. *Id.*

10. DEP'T OF EDUC., EDUCATOR SEXUAL MISCONDUCT: A SYNTHESIS OF EXISTING LITERATURE 39–40 (2004). One criticism of Shakeshaft's work has been that she combines sexual misconduct with sexual abuse.

11. *See* Associated Press, *supra* note 1.

12. *Id.*

13. W. Va. Code §18A-3-10 (2007) (passed in 2001, the statute applies only to the initial certification of teachers as of Jan. 1, 2002).

14. E-mail from Roy Einreinhofer, National Association of State Directors of Teacher Education, Executive Director, to Jennifer Blecher, Research Assistant to the author (Sept. 1, 2007, 04:15:00). ("The NASDTEC Clearinghouse is open only to jurisdictional agencies responsible for educator certification.")

15. *See* DEP'T OF EDUC., *supra* note 10, at 44.

16. CHILD SEXUAL ABUSE AND PUBLIC OPINION IN MASSACHUSETTS, Apr. 5, 2003, http://www.masskids.org (follow "Massachusetts Kids Count" hyperlink; then follow "Polling Center" hyperlink).

17. Illinois Federation of Teachers Legislative Platform, http://www.ift-aft.org/index.php (highlight "Legislative" hyperlink; then follow "Legislative Platform" hyperlink) (last visited Aug. 24, 2007).

18. *Id.*

19. Joe Feuerherd, *Crisis in Church: Maryland Senate Considers Bill to Aid Child Sex Abuse Victims*, NAT'L CATHOLIC REP., Mar. 7, 2003, *available at* http://natcath.org/NCR_Online/archives2/2003a/030703/030703e.htm.

20. *See* Allen Cowling, Defense Attorney's Ego, Conviction for the Falsely Accused, Doing It Their Way, http://www.allencowling.com/lawego.htm (last visited Aug. 28, 2007).
21. Comments of the Public Defender Service for the District of Columbia concerning Child Abduction Prevention Act H.R. 1104 Before the Subcomm. on Crime, Terrorism and Homeland Security (Mar. 11, 2003) (presented by Ronald S. Sullivan Jr., Director, American Council of Chief Defenders), *available at* http://judiciary.house.gov/media/pdfs/sullivan031103.pdf.
22. *See* Raised Bill No. 7269: An Act Concerning Criminal History Background Checks, Child Pornography, Repeated False Alarms and the Destruction of Seized Fireworks. The Statute of Limitations for Prosecution of Certain Sexual Offenses Using DNA Evidence: Hearing Before the Judiciary Comm. (2007) (statement of Deborah Del Prete Sullivan, Legal Counsel, Office of the Chief Public Defender) (opposing the proposed elimination of a statute of limitations on sexual assault offenses), *available at* http://www.ocpd.state.ct.us/Content/Leg2007/Bill/Bill_7269.pdf ("Consistent with its position in the past, the Office of Chief Public Defender would urge this committee not to support *H.B. 7085, An Act Concerning the Statute of Limitations for Prosecution of Certain Sexual Offenses Using DNA Evidence.* The proposed bill would eliminate the statute of limitations for the offenses of *C.G.S. §53a-70, Sexual Assault in the first degree, Class B or A felony; C.G.S. §53a-70a, Aggravated Sexual assault in the first degree, Class B or A felony; C.G.S. §53a-70b, Sexual assault in spousal or cohabiting relationship, Class B felony; C.G.S. §53a-71, Sexual Assault in the second degree, Class C or B felony; C.G.S. §53a-72a, Sexual Assault in the third degree, Class D or C felony;* and, *C.G.S. §53a-72b, Sexual Assault in the third degree with a firearm, Class C or B felony.*").
23. *Id.*
24. Janet Wilson & Steve Chawkins, *Letter From Bishops Draws Mixed Reactions*, L.A. TIMES, Dec. 9, 2002, at California Metro, page 4.

25. *See* Feuerherd, *supra* note 19.

26. Letter from Stephen M. Block, Legislative Counsel to The Honorable Phil Mendelson, Chairperson, Comm. on Pub. Safety and the Judiciary, *available at* http://www.aclu-nca.org/pdf/StatuteLimitationsChildAbuse6-7-07.pdf (letter entitled, Re: Bill 17–146, the "Childhood Sexual Abuse Prevention Amendment Act of 2007").

27. Beth Miller, *Senate OKs Amended Child Sexual Abuse Bill*, NEWS JOURNAL (Wilmington, Del.), June 21, 2007, at B1.

28. *See* Feuerherd, *supra* note 19.

29. Adam Jadhav, *Ruling in Clergy Abuse May Yield New Cases*, ST. LOUIS POST-DISPATCH, July 26, 2004, at B1.

## Conclusion

1. *See, e.g.*, *Morse v. Frederick*, 127 S. Ct. 2618 (2007) (ACLU supporting a student's right to free speech in a school).

2. Paul Dymit, *Child Sexual Abuse Is a Societal Problem Not Owned by Any One Institution*, MONTICELLO TIMES (Minnesota), Aug. 22, 2007, *available at* http://www.monticellotimes.com/articles/2007/08/22/opinion/editorials_-_viewpoint/68guestedabuse8237.txt.

3. One study has shown that in Minnesota alone, the cost of sexual violence was $8 billion in 2005. *See* http://www.health.state.mn.us/injury/pub/MN_brochure21FINALtoWeb.pdf.

# Index

# Index

# Index

# Index